Copycat
RESTAURANT
FAVORITES

TASTE OF HOME BOOKS • RDA ENTHUSIAST BRANDS, LLC • MILWAUKEE, WI

Taste of Home

© 2020 RDA Enthusiast Brands, LLC.
1610 N. 2nd St., Suite 102, Milwaukee WI 53212-3906
All rights reserved. Taste of Home is a registered
trademark of RDA Enthusiast Brands, LLC.
Visit us at tasteofhome.com for other Taste of Home
books and products.

ISBN: 978-1-61765-898-3
LOCC: 2019904321

Component Number: 116700091H

Deputy Editor: Mark Hagen
Senior Art Director: Raeann Thompson
Art Director: Maggie Conners
Designer: Arielle Jardine
Copy Chief: Deb Mulvey
Cover Photographer: Dan Roberts
Cover Set Stylist: Stephanie Marchese
Cover Food Stylist: Shannon Norris

Pictured on front cover:
Cheesy Broccoli Soup in a Bread Bowl, p. 49

Pictured on title page:
Garlic Lemon Shrimp, p. 57

Pictured on back cover:
Bacon Cheddar Potato Skins, p. 27;
Dulce de Leche Cheesecake, p. 107;
Fantastic Fish Tacos, p. 63

Printed in China
5 7 9 10 8 6

TABLE OF CONTENTS

Dig in to the flavor and fun of today's most popular restaurant dishes when you cook from the fantastic all-new collection **Taste of Home Copycat Restaurant Favorites.** Want to learn the secrets behind the menu items you crave most? Take a look inside and you'll discover how to whip up those dishes in your own kitchen.

From eye-opening morning staples and savory weeknight dinners to bakeshop specialties and classic desserts, you'll find the perfect recipe here. Save money, skip the drive-thru and enjoy the mouthwatering delights found on today's menus from the comfort of your own home. It's easy with this edition of **Copycat Restaurant Favorites.**

GET SOCIAL WITH US

 LIKE US: facebook.com/tasteofhome | **PIN US:** pinterest.com/taste_of_home
 FOLLOW US: @tasteofhome | **TWEET US:** twitter.com/tasteofhome

TO FIND A RECIPE:
tasteofhome.com

TO SUBMIT A RECIPE:
tasteofhome.com/submit

TO FIND OUT ABOUT OTHER
***TASTE OF HOME* PRODUCTS:**
shoptasteofhome.com

Eye-Opening Breakfasts

YOU LOVE YOUR LOCAL PANCAKE HOUSE AND DOUGHNUT SHOP, BUT NOW YOU CAN SKIP THE WAIT BY MAKING YOUR OWN VERSION AT HOME. THESE TAKES ON RESTAURANT FAVES ALWAYS START THE DAY OFF RIGHT!

COFFEE-GLAZED DOUGHNUTS, P. 11
INSPIRED BY: DUNKIN' DONUTS'
GLAZED DONUT

EGG BURRITOS

When I start with a real breakfast, I stave off hunger all day. One way to do that is to zap one of these frozen burritos in the microwave. This recipe is my family's favorite combo, but I sometimes use breakfast sausage instead of bacon.
—Audra Niederman, Aberdeen, SD

- -

TAKES: 25 min. • **MAKES:** 10 burritos

12	bacon strips, chopped
12	large eggs
½	tsp. salt
¼	tsp. pepper
10	flour tortillas (8 in.), warmed
1½	cups shredded cheddar cheese
4	green onions, thinly sliced

1. In a large cast-iron or other heavy skillet, cook bacon until crisp; drain on paper towels. Remove all but 1-2 Tbsp. drippings from pan.

2. Whisk together eggs, salt and pepper. Heat skillet over medium heat; pour in egg mixture. Cook and stir until eggs are thickened and no liquid egg remains; remove from heat.

3. Spoon about ¼ cup egg mixture onto center of each tortilla; sprinkle with cheese, bacon and green onions. Roll into burritos.

FREEZE OPTION: Cool eggs before making burritos. Individually wrap burritos in paper towels and foil; freeze in an airtight container. To use, remove foil; place paper towel-wrapped burrito on a microwave-safe plate. Microwave on high until heated through, turning once. Let stand 15 seconds.

1 BURRITO: 376 cal., 20g fat (8g sat. fat), 251mg chol., 726mg sod., 29g carb. (0 sugars, 2g fiber), 19g pro.

HEALTH TIP: Breakfast burritos can be a smart choice to start the day because they include lots of protein. To make these healthier, use whole wheat tortillas, skip the bacon, reduce the cheese and add more veggies.

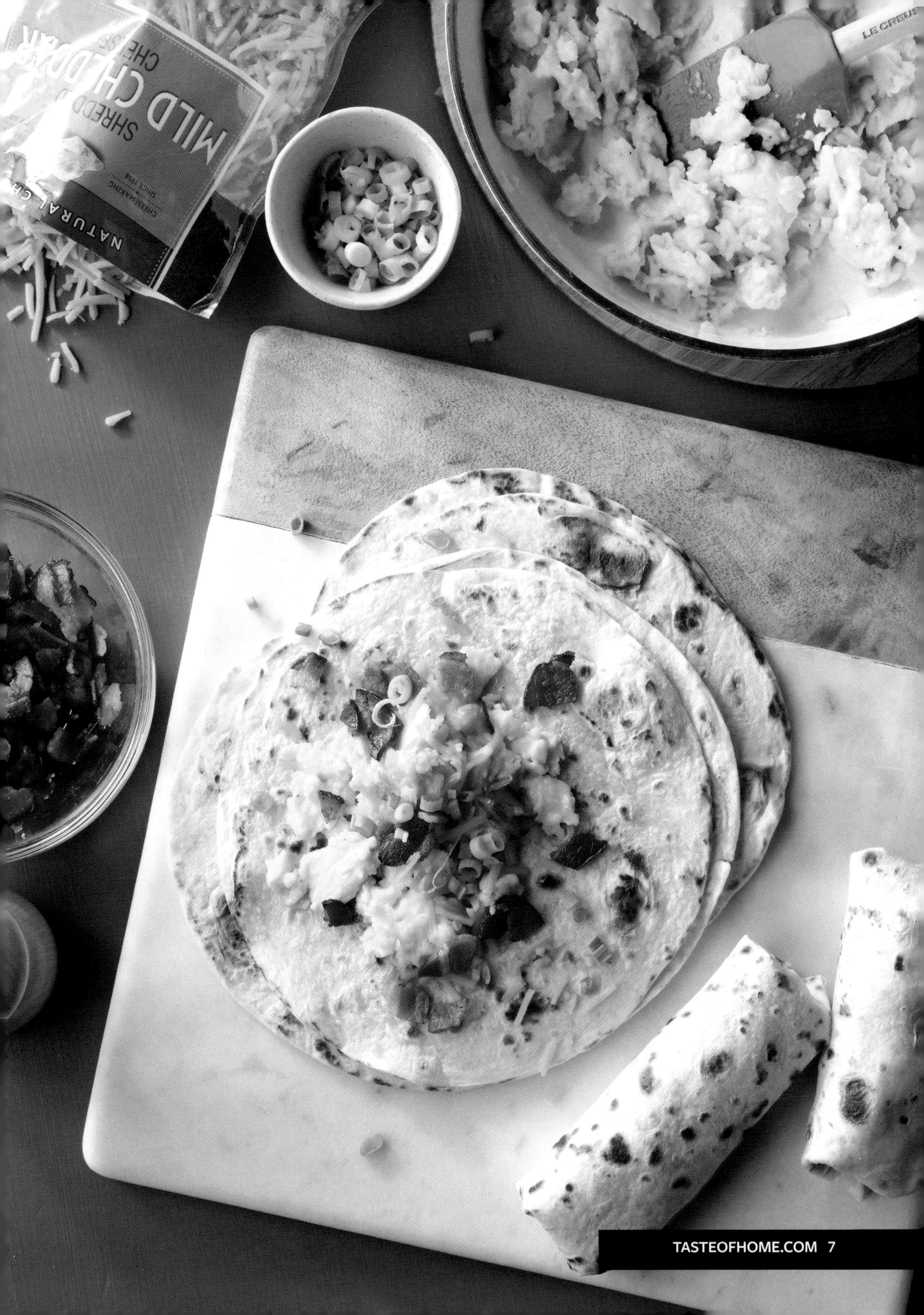
MILD CHEDDAR

INSPIRED BY:
ORANGE JULIUS'
ORANGE ORIGINAL

MORNING ORANGE DRINK

I love to treat my overnight guests to this creamy orange frappe.
Just throw a few basic ingredients in your blender and enjoy.
—Joyce Mummau, Mount Airy, MD

- -

TAKES: 10 min. • **MAKES:** 6 servings

    1   can (6 oz.) frozen orange juice concentrate
    1   cup cold water
    1   cup whole milk
    ⅓   cup sugar
    1   tsp. vanilla extract
    10 ice cubes

Combine the first 5 ingredients in a blender; process at high speed. Add ice
cubes, a few at a time, blending until smooth. Serve immediately.
¾ CUP: 115 cal., 1g fat (1g sat. fat), 6mg chol., 21mg sod., 24g carb.
(23g sugars, 0 fiber), 2g pro.

BISCUITS & SAUSAGE GRAVY

Here is my adaptation of an old southern classic. It's the kind of hearty breakfast that will warm you right up.
—Sue Baker, Jonesboro, AR

INSPIRED BY:
CRACKER BARREL'S
BISCUITS N' GRAVY

TAKES: 15 min. • **MAKES:** 2 servings

- ¼ lb. bulk pork sausage
- 2 Tbsp. butter
- 2 to 3 Tbsp. all-purpose flour
- ¼ tsp. salt
- ⅛ tsp. pepper
- 1¼ to 1⅓ cups whole milk
  Warm biscuits

In a small skillet, cook sausage over medium heat until no longer pink; drain. Add butter and heat until melted. Add the flour, salt and pepper; cook and stir until blended. Gradually add the milk, stirring constantly. Bring to a boil; cook and stir until thickened, about 2 minutes. Serve with biscuits.

¾ CUP GRAVY: 337 cal., 27g fat (14g sat. fat), 72mg chol., 718mg sod., 14g carb. (8g sugars, 0 fiber), 10g pro.

COFFEE-GLAZED DOUGHNUTS

The coffee-flavored glaze on these tasty doughnuts makes them a perfect start to any morning. You'll find that the recipe is a delectable way to use up leftover potatoes, too.
—Pat Siebenaler, Random Lake, WI

INSPIRED BY:
DUNKIN' DONUTS'
GLAZED DONUT

PREP: 25 min. + rising • **COOK:** 5 min./batch • **MAKES:** about 4 dozen

- 1 medium potato, peeled and cubed
- 2 pkg. (¼ oz. each) active dry yeast
- ¼ cup warm water (110° to 115°)
- 2 cups warm 2% milk (110° to 115°)
- ½ cup butter, softened
- 3 large eggs
- ½ tsp. lemon extract, optional
- 1 cup sugar
- 1½ tsp. salt
- ½ tsp. ground cinnamon
- 9¼ to 9¾ cups all-purpose flour

COFFEE GLAZE

- 6 to 8 Tbsp. cold 2% milk
- 1 Tbsp. instant coffee granules
- 2 tsp. vanilla extract
- ¾ cup butter, softened
- 6 cups confectioners' sugar
- ½ tsp. ground cinnamon
- Dash salt
- Oil for deep-fat frying

1. Place potato in a medium saucepan; add water to cover. Bring to a boil. Reduce heat; cook, uncovered, until tender, 8-10 minutes. Drain potatoes; return to pan. Mash until very smooth.

2. In a large bowl, dissolve yeast in warm water. Add milk, butter, potato, eggs and, if desired, extract. Add sugar, salt, cinnamon and 3 cups flour. Beat until smooth. Stir in enough remaining flour to form a soft dough. Cover and let rise in a warm place until doubled, about 1 hour.

3. Stir down dough. On a well-floured surface, roll out to ½-in. thickness. Cut with a floured 2½-in. doughnut cutter. Place on greased baking sheets; cover and let rise for 45 minutes.

4. Meanwhile, for glaze, combine 6 Tbsp. milk, coffee and vanilla; stir to dissolve coffee. In a large bowl, beat butter, sugar, cinnamon and salt. Gradually add milk mixture; beat until smooth, adding milk to reach a good dipping consistency.

5. In an electric skillet or deep-fat fryer, heat oil to 375°. Fry doughnuts, a few at a time, until golden, about 1½ minutes per side. Drain on paper towels. Dip tops in glaze while warm.

1 DOUGHNUT: 281 cal., 13g fat (4g sat. fat), 25mg chol., 127mg sod., 39g carb. (20g sugars, 1g fiber), 4g pro.

CINNAMON-SUGAR DOUGHNUTS: Omit glaze. Gently roll warm doughnuts in a mixture of 2 cups sugar and 1 tsp. ground cinnamon.

POPPY SEED DOUGHNUTS: Add ¼ cup poppy seeds to dough along with the sugar. Substitute vanilla glaze for coffee glaze. In a saucepan, bring ½ cup sugar, ¼ cup 2% milk and ¼ cup butter to a boil. Cook and stir for 1 minute. Remove from heat; cool completely. Stir in ½ cup confectioners' sugar and ¼ tsp. each salt and vanilla until smooth. Drizzle over doughnuts.

HAVE IT YOUR WAY
Drizzle a second glaze over already dipped doughnuts. Or add jimmies, chopped nuts, bacon—any topper you crave!

INSPIRED BY:
IHOP'S
GINGERBREAD PANCAKES

EASY GINGERBREAD PANCAKES

Simple yet scrumptious, these taste more like cake than breakfast pancakes. When I want to eat lighter, I top them with applesauce instead of butter and syrup.

—Trina Stewart, Yacolt, WA

PREP: 5 min. • **COOK:** 5 min./batch • **MAKES:** 12 pancakes

- 2 **cups complete pancake mix**
- 4 **tsp. molasses**
- ½ **tsp. ground cinnamon**
- ½ **tsp. ground ginger**
- ⅛ **tsp. ground cloves**
- 1½ **cups water**
  Maple syrup, optional

1. In a small bowl, combine the pancake mix, molasses, cinnamon, ginger and cloves. Stir in water just until dry ingredients are moistened.

2. Pour batter by ¼ cupfuls onto a greased hot griddle; turn when bubbles form on top. Cook until the second side is golden brown. Serve with syrup if desired.

3 PANCAKES: 248 cal., 2g fat (0 sat. fat), 0 chol., 972mg sod., 54g carb. (10g sugars, 1g fiber), 5g pro.

COUNTRY-STYLE SCRAMBLED EGGS

I added extra colors and flavors to ordinary scrambled eggs with green pepper, onion and red potatoes.

—Joyce Platfoot, Wapakoneta, OH

INSPIRED BY:
COUNTRY KITCHEN'S
FARM SKILLET

TAKES: 30 min. • **MAKES:** 4 servings

- 8 bacon strips, diced
- 2 cups diced red potatoes
- ½ cup chopped onion
- ½ cup chopped green pepper
- 8 large eggs
- ¼ cup whole milk
- 1 tsp. salt
- ¼ tsp. pepper
- 1 cup shredded cheddar cheese

1. In a 9-in. cast-iron or other ovenproof skillet, cook bacon over medium heat until crisp. Using a slotted spoon, remove to paper towels to drain. Cook and stir potatoes in drippings over medium heat for 12 minutes or until tender. Add onion and green pepper. Cook and stir for 3-4 minutes or until crisp-tender; drain. Stir in bacon.

2. In a large bowl, whisk the eggs, milk, salt and pepper; add to skillet. Cook and stir until eggs are completely set. Sprinkle with cheese; stir it in or let stand until melted.

1 SERVING: 577 cal., 45g fat (19g sat. fat), 487mg chol., 1230mg sod., 18g carb. (4g sugars, 2g fiber), 25g pro.

Coffee Shop Favorites

LOVE YOUR FAVORITE MORNING
PICK-ME-UP BUT NOT THE PRICE? SAY
GOODBYE TO EXPENSIVE CAFES AND
HELLO TO YOUR OWN HOMEMADE
COFFEE DRINKS! AND DON'T FORGET A
SWEET BAKED TREAT TO GO WITH IT.

ICED COFFEE, P. 20
INSPIRED BY: DUNKIN' DONUTS'
ICED COFFEE WITH MOCHA
FLAVOR SWIRL

HAZELNUT MOCHA FRAPPUCCINO

This smooth blend of coffee, cocoa and nutty flavors is better than any coffeehouse version we've tried. Try it, and we're sure you will agree.
—*Taste of Home* Test Kitchen

TAKES: 10 min. • **MAKES:** 3 servings

- 1 **cup whole milk**
- ½ **cup Nutella**
- 4 **tsp. instant espresso powder**
- 6 **ice cubes**
- 2 **cups vanilla ice cream**
  Chocolate curls, optional

In a blender, combine the milk, Nutella and espresso powder; cover and process until blended. Add ice cubes; cover and process until smooth. Add ice cream; cover and process until smooth. Pour into chilled glasses; serve immediately. Garnish with chocolate curls if desired.

1 CUP: 474 cal., 27g fat (10g sat. fat), 47mg chol., 124mg sod., 55g carb. (46g sugars, 2g fiber), 9g pro.

PUMPKIN SPICE LATTE

Each sip of this spiced-just-right beverage from our very own baristas tastes like a piece of pumpkin pie!

—*Taste of Home* Test Kitchen

INSPIRED BY:
STARBUCKS'
PUMPKIN SPICE LATTE

TAKES: 20 min. • **MAKES:** 6 servings

- 3 cups 2% milk
- ¾ cup canned pumpkin
- ⅓ cup packed brown sugar
- ½ tsp. ground cinnamon
- ¼ tsp. ground ginger
- ⅛ tsp. ground nutmeg
- 1½ cups hot brewed espresso or strong brewed dark roast coffee
  Whipped cream and additional nutmeg, optional

Place first 6 ingredients in a large saucepan. Cook and stir over medium heat until heated through. Stir in hot espresso. Pour into warm mugs. If desired, top with whipped cream and additional nutmeg.

1 SERVING: 124 cal., 3g fat (2g sat. fat), 10mg chol., 71mg sod., 22g carb. (19g sugars, 1g fiber), 4g pro.

ALMOND BEAR CLAWS

These bear claws are melt-in-your-mouth delicious! It's impossible to resist the delicate pastry, rich almond filling and pretty fanned tops sprinkled with sugar and almonds. I made yummy treats like this when I worked in a bakery years ago.
—Aneta Kish, La Crosse, WI

- -

PREP: 45 min. + chilling • **BAKE:** 15 min. • **MAKES:** 1½ dozen

- 1½ cups cold butter, cut into ½-in. pieces
- 5 cups all-purpose flour, divided
- 1 pkg. (¼ oz.) active dry yeast
- 1¼ cups half-and-half cream
- ¼ cup sugar
- ¼ tsp. salt
- 2 large eggs, divided use
- 1 large egg white
- ¾ cup confectioners' sugar
- ½ cup almond paste, cubed
- 1 Tbsp. water
  Sugar or coarse sugar
  Sliced almonds

1. In a bowl, toss butter with 3 cups flour until well coated; refrigerate. In a large bowl, combine yeast and remaining flour.
2. In a saucepan, heat cream, sugar and salt to 120°-130°. Add to yeast mixture with 1 egg. Beat until smooth. Stir in butter mixture just until moistened.
3. Place dough onto a well-floured surface; roll into a 21x12-in. rectangle. Starting at a short side, fold dough in thirds, forming a 12x7-in. rectangle. Give dough a quarter turn; roll into a 21x12-in. rectangle. Fold into thirds, starting with a short side. Repeat, flouring surface as needed. (Do not chill dough between each rolling and folding.) Cover and chill for 4 to 24 hours or until firm.
4. For filling, in a large bowl, beat egg white until foamy. Gradually add the confectioners' sugar and almond paste; beat until smooth. Cut dough in half widthwise. Roll each portion into a 12-in. square; cut each square into three 12x4-in. strips. Spread about 2 Tbsp. filling down center of each strip. Fold long edges together over filling; seal edges and ends. Cut into three pieces.
5. Place on parchment-lined baking sheets with folded edge facing away from you. With scissors, cut strips 4 times to within ½ in. of folded edge; separate slightly. Repeat with remaining dough and filling. Cover and let rise in a warm place until doubled, about 1 hour.
6. Lightly beat water and remaining egg; brush over dough. Sprinkle with sugar and almonds. Bake at 375° for 15 minutes or until golden brown. Remove from pans to wire racks to cool.
1 PASTRY: 352 cal., 19g fat (11g sat. fat), 73mg chol., 207mg sod., 38g carb. (10g sugars, 1g fiber), 6g pro.

INSPIRED BY:
DUNKIN' DONUTS'
ICED COFFEE WITH
MOCHA FLAVOR SWIRL

ICED COFFEE

When my sister introduced me to iced coffee, I wasn't sure I'd like it. Not only did I love it, I started making my own. This easy version is a refreshing alternative to a hot cup of joe.
—Jenny Reece, Lowry, MN

- -

TAKES: 5 min. • **MAKES:** 2 cups

- 4 tsp. instant coffee granules
- 1 cup boiling water
  Sugar substitute equivalent to 4 tsp. sugar, optional
- 1 cup fat-free milk
- 4 tsp. chocolate syrup
- ⅛ tsp. vanilla extract
  Ice cubes

In a large bowl, dissolve coffee in water. Add sweetener if desired. Stir in the milk, chocolate syrup and vanilla; mix well. Serve over ice.
NOTE: This recipe was tested with Splenda no-calorie sweetener.
1 CUP: 80 cal., 0 fat (0 sat. fat), 2mg chol., 60mg sod., 15g carb. (13g sugars, 0 fiber), 5g pro.

GINGERBREAD HOT COCOA

My spiced cocoa will put you in the Christmas spirit, no matter what time of year it is. It's like drinking a chocolate gingerbread cookie!
—Erika Monroe-Williams, Scottsdale, AZ

TAKES: 15 min. • **MAKES:** 3 servings

- ¼ cup packed brown sugar
- ¼ cup baking cocoa
- 1 Tbsp. molasses
- 1½ tsp. ground cinnamon
- 1½ tsp. ground ginger
- ½ tsp. ground allspice
  Pinch salt
- 3 cups whole milk
- 1 tsp. vanilla extract
  Whipped cream

In a small saucepan, combine the first 7 ingredients; gradually add milk. Cook and stir over medium heat until heated through. Remove from heat; stir in vanilla. Serve with whipped cream.

1 CUP: 269 cal., 9g fat (5g sat. fat), 24mg chol., 162mg sod., 41g carb. (35g sugars, 0 fiber), 9g pro.

INSPIRED BY:
IHOP'S
GINGERBREAD HOT CHOCOLATE

AUNT BETTY'S BLUEBERRY MUFFINS

My Aunt Betty is famous for her baked goods, and we especially look forward to her treats around the holidays. Her take on the classic blueberry muffin rivals that of any bakery or cafe.

—Sheila Raleigh, Kechi, KS

- -

PREP: 15 min. • **BAKE:** 20 min. • **MAKES:** about 1 dozen

½ cup old-fashioned oats
½ cup orange juice
1 large egg, room temperature
½ cup canola oil
½ cup sugar
1½ cups all-purpose flour
1¼ tsp. baking powder
½ tsp. salt
¼ tsp. baking soda
1 cup fresh or frozen blueberries

TOPPING

2 Tbsp. sugar
½ tsp. ground cinnamon

1. In a large bowl, combine oats and orange juice; let stand for 5 minutes. Beat in the egg, oil and sugar until blended. Combine the flour, baking powder, salt and baking soda; stir into oat mixture just until moistened. Fold in blueberries.

2. Fill greased or paper-lined muffin cups two-thirds full. Combine topping ingredients; sprinkle over batter. Bake at 400° for 20-25 minutes or until a toothpick inserted in the center comes out clean. Cool for 5 minutes before removing from pan to a wire rack. Serve muffins warm.

NOTE: If using frozen blueberries, use without thawing to avoid discoloring the batter.

1 MUFFIN: 208 cal., 10g fat (1g sat. fat), 18mg chol., 172mg sod., 28g carb. (13g sugars, 1g fiber), 3g pro.

INSPIRED BY:
STARBUCKS'
BLUEBERRY MUFFIN

Best Appetizers Ever

PARTY PLANNING IS A SLAM-DUNK WHEN THESE RESTAURANT-INSPIRED HOT BITES, FINGER FOODS, MUNCHIES AND MORE ARE ON THE MENU. BOOM SHAKA LAKA!

ASIAN CHICKEN DUMPLINGS, P. 35
INSPIRED BY:
CALIFORNIA PIZZA KITCHEN'S
SZECHWAN CHICKEN DUMPLINGS

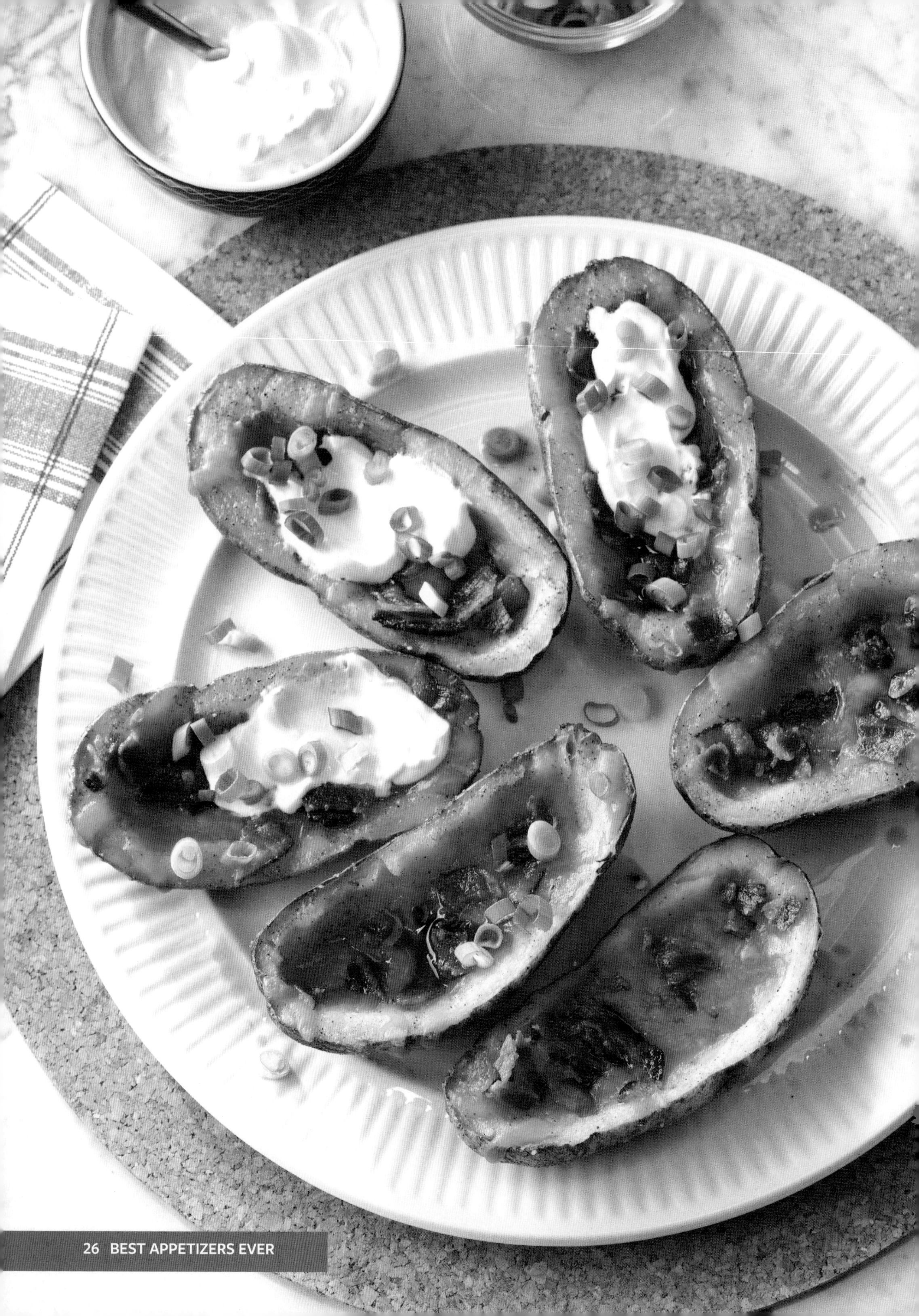

BACON CHEDDAR POTATO SKINS

Thank goodness it's tater time! My take on the classic app bakes up crisp and hearty. It's one of our family's favorites.
—Trish Perrin, Keizer, OR

- -

TAKES: 30 min. • **MAKES:** 8 servings

- 4 large baking potatoes, baked
- 3 Tbsp. canola oil
- 1 Tbsp. grated Parmesan cheese
- ½ tsp. salt
- ¼ tsp. garlic powder
- ¼ tsp. paprika
- ⅛ tsp. pepper
- 8 bacon strips, cooked and crumbled
- 1½ cups shredded cheddar cheese
- ½ cup sour cream
- 4 green onions, sliced

1. Preheat oven to 475°. Cut potatoes in half lengthwise; scoop out pulp, leaving a ¼-in. shell (save pulp for another use). Place potato skins on a greased baking sheet.
2. Combine oil with next 5 ingredients; brush over both sides of skins.
3. Bake until crisp, about 7 minutes on each side. Sprinkle bacon and cheddar cheese inside skins. Bake until cheese is melted, about 2 minutes longer. Top with sour cream and onions. Serve immediately.

1 POTATO SKIN: 350 cal., 19g fat (7g sat. fat), 33mg chol., 460mg sod., 34g carb. (2g sugars, 4g fiber), 12g pro.

INSPIRED BY:
TGI FRIDAYS'
LOADED POTATO SKINS

HAVE IT YOUR WAY
Cut down your kitchen time. Instead of prebaking the potatoes in an oven for 50-60 minutes, microwave them for 4 minutes. Scoop out the pulp, then make the potato skins as directed.

INSPIRED BY:
CALIFORNIA PIZZA KITCHEN'S
WHITE CORN GUACAMOLE + CHIPS

AVOCADO SALSA

I first served this salsa at a party, and it was a hit. People love the garlic, corn and avocado combination.
—Susan Vandermeer, Ogden, UT

PREP: 20 min. + chilling • **MAKES:** about 7 cups

1⅔ cups (about 8¼ oz.) frozen corn, thawed
2 cans (2¼ oz. each) sliced ripe olives, drained
1 medium sweet red pepper, chopped
1 small onion, chopped
5 garlic cloves, minced
⅓ cup olive oil
¼ cup lemon juice
3 Tbsp. cider vinegar
1 tsp. dried oregano
½ tsp. salt
½ tsp. pepper
4 medium ripe avocados, peeled
  Tortilla chips

1. Combine corn, olives, red pepper and chopped onion. In another bowl, mix the next 7 ingredients. Pour over corn mixture; toss to coat. Refrigerate, covered, overnight.
2. Just before serving, chop avocados; stir into salsa. Serve with tortilla chips.
¼ **CUP:** 82 cal., 7g fat (1g sat. fat), 0 chol., 85mg sod., 5g carb. (1g sugars, 2g fiber), 1g pro. **DIABETIC EXCHANGES:** 1½ fat.

HONEY-MUSTARD CHICKEN WINGS

Take a walk on the wild side with these sweet and sticky wings. They're a fun flavor twist from traditional spicy Buffalo sauce. Be warned: They may become your new favorite!
—Susan Seymour, Valatie, NY

- -

PREP: 15 min. • **BAKE:** 1 hour • **MAKES:** about 3 dozen

4	lbs. chicken wings
½	cup spicy brown mustard
½	cup honey
¼	cup butter, cubed
2	Tbsp. lemon juice
¼	tsp. ground turmeric

1. Preheat oven to 400°. Line two 15x10x1-in. baking pans with foil; grease foil. Using a sharp knife, cut through the 2 chicken wing joints; discard wing tips. Place remaining wings in prepared pans.

2. In a small saucepan, combine remaining ingredients; bring to a boil, stirring frequently. Pour over wings, turning to coat. Bake 30-40 minutes on each side or until wings are glazed and chicken juices run clear.

1 CHICKEN WING: 152 cal., 9g fat (3g sat. fat), 35mg chol., 107mg sod., 7g carb. (7g sugars, 0 fiber), 9g pro.

INSPIRED BY:
BUFFALO WILD WINGS'
BOURBON HONEY MUSTARD WINGS

SOFT GIANT PRETZELS

My husband, friends and family love these soft, chewy pretzels. Let your bread machine mix the dough; then all you have to do is shape and bake.
—Sherry Peterson, Fort Collins, CO

- -

PREP: 20 min. + rising • **BAKE:** 10 min. • **MAKES:** 8 pretzels

1	cup plus 2 Tbsp. water (70° to 80°)
3	cups all-purpose flour
3	Tbsp. brown sugar
1½	tsp. active dry yeast
2	qt. water
½	cup baking soda
	Coarse salt

1. In bread machine pan, place the first 4 ingredients in order suggested by manufacturer. Select dough setting (check dough after 5 minutes of mixing; add 1-2 Tbsp. water or flour if needed).

2. When cycle is completed, turn dough onto a lightly floured surface. Divide dough into 8 balls. Roll each into a 20-in. rope; form into pretzel shape.

3. Preheat oven to 425°. In a large saucepan, bring water and baking soda to a boil. Drop pretzels into boiling water, 2 at a time; boil for 10-15 seconds. Remove with a slotted spoon; drain on paper towels.

4. Place pretzels on greased baking sheets. Bake until golden brown, 8-10 minutes. Spritz or lightly brush with water. Sprinkle with salt.

1 PRETZEL: 193 cal., 1g fat (0 sat. fat), 0 chol., 380mg sod., 41g carb. (5g sugars, 1g fiber), 5g pro.

PEPPERMINT POPCORN

Crisp and minty, this simple snack is a hit with all 10 of our children. For variety, try substituting other flavors of candy for the peppermint.
—Shirley Mars, Kent, OH

PREP: 10 min. • **MAKES:** 24 servings

- 1 lb. white candy coating, coarsely chopped
- 24 cups popped popcorn
- ½ to ¾ cup finely crushed peppermint candy (4 to 6 candy canes)
  Red nonpareils, optional

In a microwave, melt candy coating; stir until smooth. In a large bowl, combine the popcorn and crushed candy. Pour candy coating over top; toss to coat. Pour onto a waxed paper-lined baking sheet. If desired, sprinkle with nonpareils. When hardened, break apart. Store in an airtight container.
1 CUP: 163 cal., 8g fat (5g sat. fat), 0 chol., 98mg sod., 22g carb. (14g sugars, 1g fiber), 1g pro.

TOMATO FRITTERS

I got the basic recipe for these fritters from a friend, then I tweaked it for my family's tastes. It's one of our favorite appetizers in summer. We love them right after they've been fried, when they're still hot and crispy.
—Pam Halter, Bridgeton, NJ

PREP: 15 min. • **COOK:** 5 min./batch • **MAKES:** about 2½ dozen

- 1 cup all-purpose flour
- 1 tsp. baking powder
- ½ tsp. salt
- Dash dried basil
- Dash dried oregano
- Dash pepper
- 1 large tomato, finely chopped
- ½ cup chopped onion
- ½ cup shredded Parmesan cheese
- 1 jalapeno pepper, seeded and finely chopped
- 1 garlic clove, minced
- 1 to 6 Tbsp. water, optional
- Oil for deep-fat frying

1. In a large bowl, whisk flour, baking powder, salt, basil, oregano and pepper. Gently stir in tomato, onion, cheese, jalapeno and garlic just until moistened. If the batter seems thick, add water 1 Tbsp. at a time to thin it slightly until it loosens up and mixes easily.

2. In a cast-iron or other heavy skillet, heat oil to 375°. Drop batter by rounded tablespoonfuls, a few at a time, into hot oil. Fry until golden brown, about 1½ minutes per side. Drain on paper towels.

1 FRITTER: 40 cal., 2g fat (0 sat. fat), 1mg chol., 79mg sod., 4g carb. (0 sugars, 0 fiber), 1g pro.

INSPIRED BY:
TEXAS ROADHOUSE'S
RATTLESNAKE BITES

HAVE IT YOUR WAY

The water in this recipe is optional. It will depend on how ripe and juicy your tomatoes are. Fry one fritter as a test. If the middle is still undercooked when the exterior is golden brown, add some water to the batter to loosen it and make a slightly thinner fritter.

ASIAN CHICKEN DUMPLINGS

We occasionally make Chinese food to celebrate our two daughters' heritage, especially around holidays like the Lunar New Year. I took a traditional pork dumpling recipe and modified it to use ground chicken. Feel free to sprinkle cilantro, sesame seeds or scallions on top for extra flair.

—Joy Olcott, Millersville, PA

- -

PREP: 40 min. • **COOK:** 10 min./batch • **MAKES:** 2½ dozen

1	lb. ground chicken
4	green onions, chopped
½	cup chopped cabbage
¼	cup minced fresh cilantro
2	tsp. minced fresh gingerroot
1	tsp. salt
¼	tsp. Chinese five-spice powder
2	Tbsp. water
1	pkg. (10 oz.) pot sticker or gyoza wrappers
	Cabbage leaves
	Reduced-sodium soy sauce

1. Place the first 7 ingredients in a food processor; cover and process until finely chopped. Add water; cover and process until blended.

2. Place 1 Tbsp. chicken mixture in the center of 1 wrapper. (Keep remaining wrappers covered with a damp paper towel to prevent them from drying out.) Moisten edges with water. Fold wrapper over filling to form a semicircle; press edges firmly to seal, pleating the front side to form 3 to 5 folds.

3. Holding sealed edges, stand each dumpling on an even surface; press to flatten bottom. Repeat with remaining wrappers and filling; cover dumplings with plastic wrap.

4. Line a steamer basket with 4 cabbage leaves. Arrange the dumplings in batches 1 in. apart over cabbage; place in a large saucepan over 1 in. of water. Bring to a boil; cover and steam for 10-12 minutes or until a thermometer reads 165°. Discard cabbage leaves. Repeat. Serve with soy sauce.

1 DUMPLING: 45 cal., 1g fat (0 sat. fat), 10mg chol., 109mg sod., 6g carb. (0 sugars, 0 fiber), 3g pro.

INSPIRED BY:
P.F. CHANG'S
CHICKEN MINI EGG ROLLS

BAKED EGG ROLLS

These baked beauties are low in fat, but their crisp baked texture will fool you into thinking they're fried! Serve with your favorite Asian dipping sauce.
—Barbara Lierman, Lyons, NE

PREP: 30 min. • **BAKE:** 10 min. • **MAKES:** 8 servings

- 2 cups grated carrots
- 1 can (14 oz.) bean sprouts, drained
- ½ cup chopped water chestnuts
- ¼ cup chopped green pepper
- ¼ cup chopped green onions
- 1 garlic clove, minced
- 2 cups finely diced cooked chicken
- 4 tsp. cornstarch
- 1 Tbsp. water
- 1 Tbsp. light soy sauce
- 1 tsp. canola oil
- 1 tsp. brown sugar
  Pinch cayenne pepper
- 16 egg roll wrappers
  Cooking spray

1. Coat a large skillet with cooking spray; add the first 6 ingredients. Cook and stir over medium heat until vegetables are crisp-tender, about 3 minutes. Add chicken; heat through.
2. In a small bowl, combine the cornstarch, water, soy sauce, oil, brown sugar and cayenne until smooth; stir into chicken mixture. Bring to a boil. Cook and stir for 2 minutes or until thickened; remove from the heat.
3. Spoon ¼ cup chicken mixture on the bottom third of 1 egg roll wrapper; fold sides toward center and roll tightly. (Keep remaining wrappers covered with a damp paper towel until ready to use.) Place seam side down on a baking sheet coated with cooking spray. Repeat.
4. Spritz tops of egg rolls with cooking spray. Bake at 425° for 10-15 minutes or until lightly browned.
FREEZE OPTION: Freeze cooled egg rolls in a freezer container, separating layers with waxed paper. To use, reheat rolls on a baking sheet in a preheated 350° oven until crisp and heated through.
2 EGG ROLLS: 261 cal., 3g fat (0 sat. fat), 27mg chol., 518mg sod., 45g carb. (0 sugars, 0 fiber), 13g pro.
EFFORTLESS EGG ROLLS: Thaw and chop 1 lb. frozen stir-fry vegetable blend; cook in a large skillet with 1 lb. bulk pork sausage until meat is no longer pink. Stir in 2 Tbsp. teriyaki sauce. Fill and bake egg rolls as directed.

Specialty
Soups, Salads &
Sandwiches

EAT THEM ON THEIR OWN, OR PAIR 'EM UP—THE RECIPES IN THIS CHAPTER LET YOU MIX AND MATCH SOUPS, SANDWICHES AND SALADS FROM YOUR FAVORITE RESTAURANTS!

BACON & SWISS CHICKEN SANDWICHES, P. 50
INSPIRED BY: APPLEBEE'S
BACON CHEDDAR GRILLED
CHICKEN SANDWICH

INSPIRED BY:
APPLEBEE'S
QUESADILLA BURGER

FAJITA BURGER WRAPS

This tasty combo gives you a tender burger and crisp veggies in a crunchy shell, plus fajita flavor. Kids just love it!
—Antonio Smith, Canal Winchester, OH

TAKES: 30 min. • **MAKES:** 4 servings

1	**lb. lean ground beef (90% lean)**
2	**Tbsp. fajita seasoning mix**
2	**tsp. canola oil**
1	**medium green pepper, cut into thin strips**
1	**medium red sweet pepper, cut into thin strips**
1	**medium onion, halved and sliced**
4	**flour tortillas (10 in.)**
¾	**cup shredded cheddar cheese**

1. In a large bowl, combine beef and seasoning mix, mixing lightly but thoroughly. Shape into four ½-in.-thick patties.
2. In a large skillet, heat oil over medium heat. Add burgers; cook 4 minutes on each side. Remove from pan. In the same skillet, add peppers and onion; cook and stir 5-7 minutes or until lightly browned and tender.
3. On the center of each tortilla, place ½ cup pepper mixture, 1 burger and 3 Tbsp. cheese. Fold sides of tortilla over burger; fold top and bottom to close, forming a square.
4. Wipe skillet clean. Place wraps in skillet, seam side down. Cook over medium heat for 1-2 minutes on each side or until golden brown and a thermometer inserted in the beef reads 160°.
1 WRAP: 533 cal., 23g fat (9g sat. fat), 92mg chol., 1190mg sod., 45g carb. (5g sugars, 3g fiber), 34g pro.

GARDEN-FRESH CHEF SALAD

For much of the year, I can use my garden's produce when I make this cool salad. In spring, it's mixed greens and radishes, and in summer, we have tomatoes, cabbage and carrots. What a good feeling!
—Evelyn Gubernath, Bucyrus, OH

INSPIRED BY:
MCALISTER'S DELI
CHEF SALAD

TAKES: 25 min. • **MAKES:** 6 servings

- 6 cups spring mix salad greens
- 2 medium tomatoes, coarsely chopped
- 6 hard-boiled large eggs, coarsely chopped
- 3 slices deli turkey, cut into thin strips
- 3 slices deli ham, cut into thin strips
- ½ cup shredded cabbage
- 4 green onions, sliced
- 4 fresh baby carrots, sliced
- 4 radishes, thinly sliced
- ¼ tsp. garlic powder
- ¼ tsp. pepper
- ½ cup reduced-fat Thousand Island salad dressing or dressing of your choice

In a large bowl, combine the first 9 ingredients. Sprinkle with garlic powder and pepper; toss to coat. Serve with salad dressing.

2 CUPS: 171 cal., 9g fat (2g sat. fat), 227mg chol., 508mg sod., 11g carb. (6g sugars, 2g fiber), 12g pro.
DIABETIC EXCHANGES: 2 lean meat, 2 vegetable, 1 fat.

STRAWBERRY SALAD WITH POPPY SEED DRESSING

My family is always happy to see this fruit and veggie salad. If strawberries aren't available, substitute mandarin oranges and dried cranberries.
—Irene Keller, Kalamazoo, MI

TAKES: 30 min. • **MAKES:** 10 servings

- ¼ cup sugar
- ⅓ cup slivered almonds
- 1 bunch romaine, torn (about 8 cups)
- 1 small onion, halved and thinly sliced
- 2 cups halved fresh strawberries

DRESSING
- ¼ cup mayonnaise
- 2 Tbsp. sugar
- 1 Tbsp. sour cream
- 1 Tbsp. 2% milk
- 2¼ tsp. cider vinegar
- 1½ tsp. poppy seeds

1. Place sugar in a small heavy skillet; cook and stir over medium-low heat until melted and caramel colored, about 10 minutes. Stir in almonds until coated. Spread on foil to cool.

2. Place romaine, onion and strawberries in a large bowl. Whisk together dressing ingredients; toss with salad. Break candied almonds into pieces; sprinkle over salad. Serve immediately.

¾ CUP: 110 cal., 6g fat (1g sat. fat), 1mg chol., 33mg sod., 13g carb. (10g sugars, 2g fiber), 2g pro.
DIABETIC EXCHANGES: ½ starch, 1 vegetable, 1 fat.

HAVE IT YOUR WAY
Turn this side salad into something heartier. Grill 2 pounds boneless skinless chicken breasts, slice, and add to the salad for 10 main-dish servings.

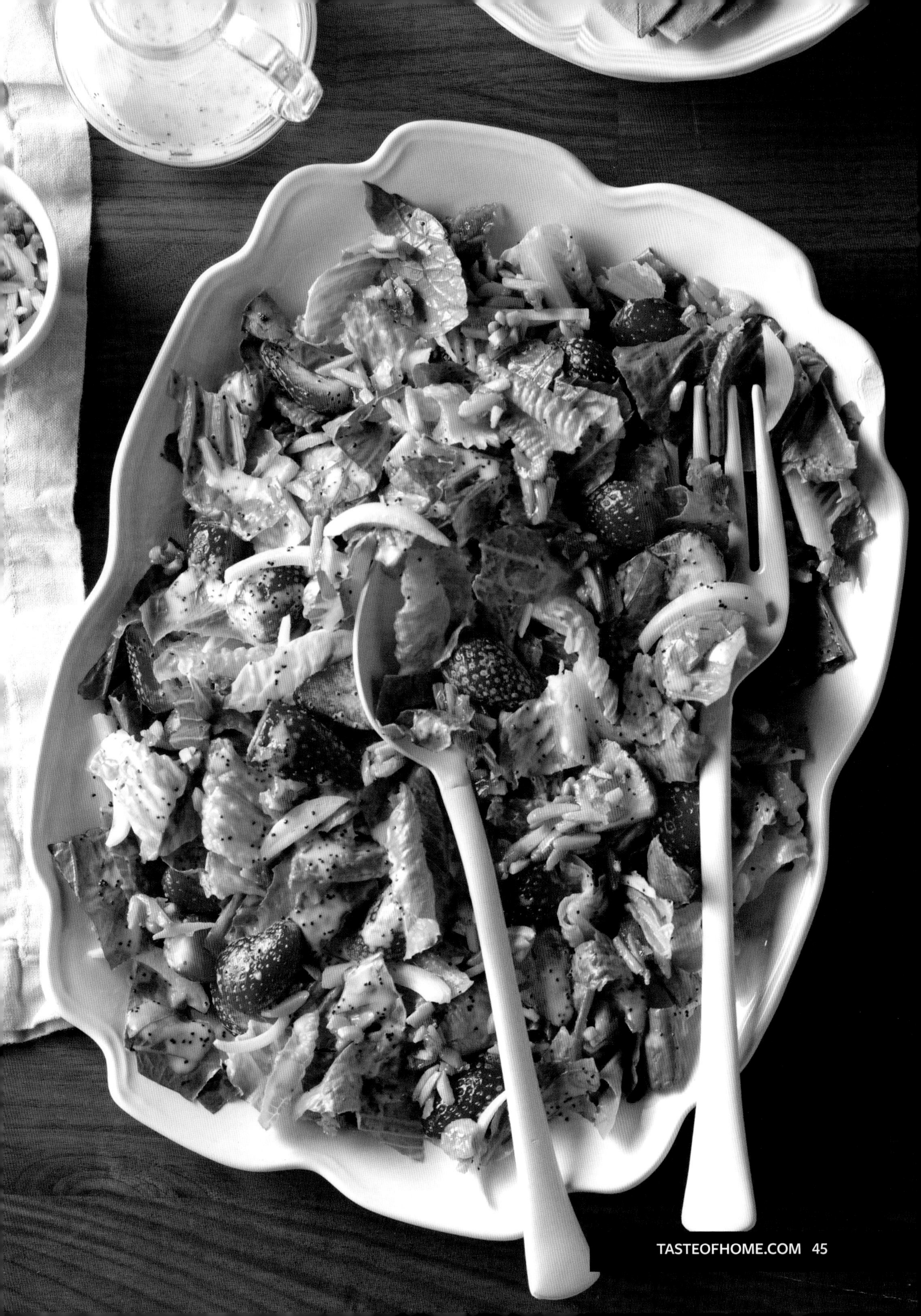

INSPIRED BY:
OLIVE GARDEN'S
PASTA E FAGIOLI

HEARTY PASTA FAGIOLI

Here's a classic Italian favorite. Spaghetti sauce and canned broth form the flavorful base of this satisfying soup.
—Cindy Garland, Limestone, TN

PREP: 40 min. • **COOK:** 40 min. • **MAKES:** 24 servings (7½ qt.)

- 2 lbs. ground beef
- 6 cans (14½ oz. each) beef broth
- 2 cans (28 oz. each) diced tomatoes, undrained
- 2 jars (26 oz. each) spaghetti sauce
- 3 large onions, chopped
- 8 celery ribs, diced
- 3 medium carrots, sliced
- 1 can (16 oz.) kidney beans, rinsed and drained
- 1 can (15 oz.) cannellini beans, rinsed and drained
- 3 tsp. minced fresh oregano or 1 tsp. dried oregano
- 2½ tsp. pepper
- 1½ tsp. hot pepper sauce
- 8 oz. uncooked medium pasta shells
- 5 tsp. minced fresh parsley

1. In a large stockpot, cook beef over medium heat until no longer pink; drain. Add broth, tomatoes, spaghetti sauce, onions, celery, carrots, beans, oregano, pepper and pepper sauce.
2. Bring to a boil. Reduce heat; simmer, covered, 30 minutes. Add pasta and parsley; simmer, covered, until pasta is tender, 10-14 minutes.
1¼ CUPS: 212 cal., 6g fat (2g sat. fat), 20mg chol., 958mg sod., 25g carb. (8g sugars, 5g fiber), 14g pro.

COPYCAT CHICKEN SALAD

This chicken salad recipe is incredibly easy to make, and your family will love it. The sweet pickle relish gives it that distinctive taste. I like to use a thick, crusty oat bread for this sandwich.
—Julie Peterson, Crofton, MD

- -

TAKES: 20 min. • **MAKES:** 2 servings

½   cup reduced-fat mayonnaise
⅓   cup sweet pickle relish
⅓   cup finely chopped celery
½   tsp. sugar
¼   tsp. salt
¼   tsp. pepper
1   hard-boiled large egg, cooled and minced
2   cups chopped cooked chicken breast
4   slices whole wheat bread, toasted
2   romaine leaves

Mix the first 7 ingredients; stir in the chicken. Line 2 slices of toast with lettuce. Top with chicken salad and the remaining toast.

1 SANDWICH: 651 cal., 29g fat (5g sat. fat), 222mg chol., 1386mg sod., 45g carb. (18g sugars, 4g fiber), 51g pro.

INSPIRED BY:
CHICK-FIL-A'S
CHICKEN SALAD

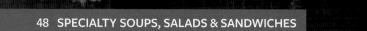

CHEESY BROCCOLI SOUP IN A BREAD BOWL

This creamy, cheesy broccoli soup tastes just like the one found at Panera Bread! My family requests it all the time. You can even make your own homemade bread bowls with the recipe on my blog, Yammie's Noshery.

—Rachel Preus, Marshall, MI

- -

PREP: 15 min. • **COOK:** 30 min. • **MAKES:** 6 servings

- ¼ cup butter, cubed
- ½ cup chopped onion
- 2 garlic cloves, minced
- 4 cups fresh broccoli florets (about 8 oz.)
- 1 large carrot, finely chopped
- 3 cups chicken stock
- 2 cups half-and-half cream
- 2 bay leaves
- ½ tsp. salt
- ¼ tsp. ground nutmeg
- ¼ tsp. pepper
- ¼ cup cornstarch
- ¼ cup water or additional chicken stock
- 2½ cups shredded cheddar cheese
- 6 small round bread loaves (about 8 oz. each), optional

1. In a 6-qt. stockpot, heat butter over medium heat; saute onion and garlic until tender, 6-8 minutes. Stir in broccoli, carrot, stock, cream and seasonings; bring to a boil. Simmer, uncovered, until vegetables are tender, 10-12 minutes.

2. Mix cornstarch and water until smooth; stir into soup. Bring to a boil, stirring occasionally; cook and stir until thickened, 1-2 minutes. Remove bay leaves. Stir in cheese until melted.

3. If using bread bowls, cut a slice off the top of each bread loaf; hollow out bottoms, leaving ¼-in.-thick shells (save the removed bread for another use). Fill with soup just before serving.

1 CUP SOUP: 422 cal., 32g fat (19g sat. fat), 107mg chol., 904mg sod., 15g carb. (5g sugars, 2g fiber), 17g pro.

INSPIRED BY:
PANERA BREAD'S
BROCCOLI CHEDDAR SOUP

HAVE IT YOUR WAY
Be a smooth operator. Avoid gritty cheese sauces by allowing the soup to cool slightly before adding the cheese. Stir in a little at a time until it melts into the soup.

INSPIRED BY:
APPLEBEE'S
BACON CHEDDAR
GRILLED CHICKEN
SANDWICH

BACON & SWISS CHICKEN SANDWICHES

I created this sandwich based on one my daughter ordered at a restaurant. She likes to dip her sandwich in the extra honey-mustard sauce.
—Marilyn Moberg, Papillion, NE

- -

TAKES: 25 min. • **MAKES:** 4 servings

- ¼ cup reduced-fat mayonnaise
- 1 Tbsp. Dijon mustard
- 1 Tbsp. honey
- 4 boneless skinless chicken breast halves (4 oz. each)
- ½ tsp. Montreal steak seasoning
- 4 slices Swiss cheese
- 4 whole wheat hamburger buns, split
- 2 bacon strips, cooked and crumbled
  Lettuce leaves and tomato slices, optional

1. In a small bowl, mix mayonnaise, mustard and honey. Pound chicken with a meat mallet to ½-in. thickness. Sprinkle chicken with steak seasoning. Grill, covered, over medium heat or broil 4 in. from heat until a thermometer reads 165°, 4-6 minutes on each side. Top chicken breasts with cheese during the last 1 minute of cooking.
2. Grill buns over medium heat, cut side down, until toasted, 30-60 seconds. Serve chicken on buns with bacon, the mayonnaise mixture and, if desired, lettuce and tomato.
1 SANDWICH: 410 cal., 17g fat (6g sat. fat), 91mg chol., 667mg sod., 29g carb. (9g sugars, 3g fiber), 34g pro.
DIABETIC EXCHANGES: 4 lean meat, 2 starch, 2 fat.

SLOW-COOKED CHILI

This hearty chili can cook for up to 10 hours on low in the slow cooker. It's so good to come home to its wonderful aroma after a long day away.
—Sue Call, Beech Grove, IN

INSPIRED BY:
WENDY'S CHILI

PREP: 20 min. • **COOK:** 8 hours • **MAKES:** 10 servings (2½ qt.)

- 2 lbs. lean ground beef (90% lean)
- 2 cans (16 oz. each) kidney beans, rinsed and drained
- 2 cans (14½ oz. each) diced tomatoes, undrained
- 1 can (8 oz.) tomato sauce
- 2 medium onions, chopped
- 1 green pepper, chopped
- 2 garlic cloves, minced
- 2 Tbsp. chili powder
- 1 tsp. salt
- 1 tsp. pepper
  Shredded cheddar cheese and thinly sliced green onions, optional

1. In a large skillet, cook beef over medium heat until no longer pink; drain.
2. Transfer to a 5-qt. slow cooker. Add the next 9 ingredients. Cover and cook on low for 8-10 hours. If desired, top individual servings with cheese and green onions.

1 CUP: 260 cal., 8g fat (3g sat. fat), 57mg chol., 712mg sod., 23g carb. (6g sugars, 7g fiber), 25g pro.
DIABETIC EXCHANGES: 3 lean meat, 1½ starch, 1 vegetable.

Copycat Entrees

DIG IN! WITH THESE COPYCAT RECIPES, IT'S A SNAP TO SERVE THE SIGNATURE DISHES FROM YOUR FAVORITE EATERIES. TURN HERE FOR CASUAL MEALS, WEEKEND SPECIALTIES AND EVERYTHING IN BETWEEN!

**WISCONSIN BUTTER-BASTED
BURGERS, P. 67**
INSPIRED BY: CULVER'S
BUTTERBURGER "THE ORIGINAL"

FLAVORFUL CHICKEN FAJITAS

The marinated chicken in these popular wraps is mouthwatering.
They go together in a snap and always get raves!
—Julie Sterchi, Campbellsville, KY

INSPIRED BY:
CHILI'S
CHICKEN FAJITAS

- -

PREP: 20 min. + marinating • **COOK:** 10 min. • **MAKES:** 6 servings

- 4 Tbsp. canola oil, divided
- 2 Tbsp. lemon juice
- 1½ tsp. seasoned salt
- 1½ tsp. dried oregano
- 1½ tsp. ground cumin
- 1 tsp. garlic powder
- ½ tsp. chili powder
- ½ tsp. paprika
- ½ tsp. crushed red pepper flakes, optional
- 1½ lbs. boneless skinless chicken breast, cut into thin strips
- ½ medium sweet red pepper, julienned
- ½ medium green pepper, julienned
- 4 green onions, thinly sliced
- ½ cup chopped onion
- 6 flour tortillas (8 in.), warmed
  Shredded cheddar cheese, taco sauce, salsa, guacamole and
  sour cream, optional

1. In a large bowl, combine 2 Tbsp. oil, lemon juice and seasonings; add the chicken. Turn to coat; cover. Refrigerate for 1-4 hours.

2. In a large skillet, saute peppers and onions in remaining oil until crisp-tender. Remove and keep warm.

3. Drain chicken, discarding marinade. In the same skillet, cook chicken over medium-high heat for 5-6 minutes or until no longer pink. Return pepper mixture to pan; heat through.

4. Spoon filling down the center of tortillas; fold in half. Serve with toppings as desired.

1 FAJITA: 369 cal., 15g fat (2g sat. fat), 63mg chol., 689mg sod., 30g carb. (2g sugars, 1g fiber), 28g pro.
DIABETIC EXCHANGES: 3 lean meat, 2 starch, 2 fat.

HAVE IT YOUR WAY
Oregano is used frequently in Latin American cuisine. Mexican oregano has a citrusy, peppery bite but it is similar in flavor to the sweeter Mediterranean oregano. Either variety works well in these lip-smacking fajitas!

INSPIRED BY:
SONIC DRIVE-IN'S
CORN DOG

INDIANA-STYLE CORN DOGS

One of the best parts of attending the many fairs and festivals in Indiana is the corn dogs! My family adores corn dogs, so I make these fairly often at home. Everyone loves them!
—Sally Denney, Warsaw, IN

- -

PREP: 20 min. • **COOK:** 5 min./batch • **MAKES:** 12 corn dogs

- 1 cup all-purpose flour
- ½ cup yellow cornmeal
- 1 Tbsp. sugar
- 3 tsp. baking powder
- 1 tsp. salt
- ½ tsp. ground mustard
- ¼ tsp. paprika
  Dash pepper
- 1 large egg, lightly beaten
- 1 cup evaporated milk
  Oil for deep-fat frying
- 12 wooden skewers
- 12 hot dogs

1. In a bowl, whisk the first 8 ingredients. Whisk in egg and milk just until blended. Transfer batter to a tall drinking glass.
2. In an electric skillet or deep-fat fryer, heat oil to 375°. Insert skewers into hot dogs. Dip hot dogs into batter; allow excess batter to drip off. Fry corn dogs, a few at a time, 2-3 minutes or until golden brown, turning occasionally. Drain on paper towels. Serve immediately.
1 CORN DOG: 299 cal., 21g fat (7g sat. fat), 47mg chol., 805mg sod., 18g carb. (4g sugars, 1 fiber), 9g pro.

GARLIC LEMON SHRIMP

This shrimp dish is amazingly quick to get on the table. Serve it with crusty bread so you can soak up the luscious garlic lemon sauce.
—Athena Russell, Greenville, SC

- -

TAKES: 20 min. • **MAKES:** 4 servings

2	Tbsp. olive oil
1	lb. uncooked shrimp (26-30 per lb.), peeled and deveined
3	garlic cloves, thinly sliced
1	Tbsp. lemon juice
1	tsp. ground cumin
¼	tsp. salt
2	Tbsp. minced fresh parsley
	Hot cooked pasta or rice

In a large skillet, heat oil over medium-high heat; saute shrimp 3 minutes. Add garlic, lemon juice, cumin and salt; cook and stir until shrimp turn pink. Stir in parsley. Serve with pasta.

1 SERVING: 163 cal., 8g fat (1g sat. fat), 138mg chol., 284mg sod., 2g carb. (0 sugars, 0 fiber), 19g pro.
DIABETIC EXCHANGES: 3 lean meat, 1½ fat.

INSPIRED BY:
TGI FRIDAYS'
**LEMON AND GARLIC
SHRIMP PASTA**

HAVE IT YOUR WAY
Cooking the shrimp in olive oil instead of butter saves about 3 grams of saturated fat per serving.

ULTIMATE POT ROAST

Pot roast is the ultimate comfort food. When this juicy pot roast simmers for hours in garlic, onions and veggies, everyone comes running to ask, "When can we eat?" The answer? Just wait—it will be worth it.
—Nick Iverson, Denver, CO

PREP: 55 min. • **BAKE:** 2 hours • **MAKES:** 8 servings

- 1 boneless beef chuck-eye or other chuck roast (3 to 4 lbs.)
- 2 tsp. pepper
- 2 tsp. salt, divided
- 2 Tbsp. canola oil
- 2 medium onions, cut into 1-in. pieces
- 2 celery ribs, chopped
- 3 garlic cloves, minced
- 1 Tbsp. tomato paste
- 1 Tbsp. minced fresh thyme or 1 tsp. dried thyme
- 2 bay leaves
- 1 cup dry red wine or reduced-sodium beef broth
- 2 cups reduced-sodium beef broth
- 1 lb. small red potatoes, quartered
- 4 medium parsnips, peeled and cut into 2-in. pieces
- 6 medium carrots, cut into 2-in. pieces
- 1 Tbsp. red wine vinegar
- 2 Tbsp. minced fresh parsley
  Salt and pepper to taste

1. Preheat oven to 325°. Pat roast dry with a paper towel; tie at 2-in. intervals with kitchen string. Sprinkle roast with pepper and 1½ tsp. salt. In a Dutch oven, heat oil over medium-high heat. Brown roast on all sides. Remove from the pan.

2. Add onions, celery and ½ tsp. salt to the same pan; cook and stir over medium heat 8-10 minutes or until onions are browned. Add garlic, tomato paste, thyme and bay leaves; cook and stir 1 minute longer.

3. Add wine, stirring to loosen browned bits from pan; stir in broth. Return roast to pan. Arrange potatoes, parsnips and carrots around roast; bring to a boil. Bake, covered, until meat is fork-tender, 2-2½ hours.

4. Remove roast and vegetables from pan; keep warm. Discard bay leaves; skim fat from cooking juices. On stovetop, bring juices to a boil; cook until liquid is reduced by half (about 1½ cups), 10-12 minutes. Stir in vinegar and parsley; season with salt and pepper to taste.

5. Remove string from roast. Serve with vegetables and sauce.

3 OZ. COOKED BEEF WITH 1 CUP VEGETABLES AND 3 TBSP. SAUCE:
459 cal., 20g fat (7g sat. fat), 112mg chol., 824mg sod., 32g carb. (8g sugars, 6g fiber), 37g pro.

HAVE IT YOUR WAY

Chuck is the ideal cut for this type of low-and-slow braising because it has plenty of marbling and collagen. This translates to tenderness and flavor! Brisket is a good choice, too. Very lean cuts like rump and round roasts will work but will not be nearly as moist and fall-apart tender.

INSPIRED BY:
CRACKER BARREL
HICKORY-SMOKED
COUNTRY HAM

COUNTRY HAM & POTATOES

Browned potatoes are a simple but perfect side for country ham. Not only do the potatoes pick up the flavor of the ham, but they look beautiful! Just add veggies or a salad and dinner's done.
—Helen Bridges, Washington, VA

- -

TAKES: 30 min. • **MAKES:** 6 servings

2   lbs. fully cooked sliced ham (about ½ in. thick)
2   to 3 Tbsp. butter
1½ lbs. potatoes, peeled, quartered and cooked
    Snipped fresh parsley

In a large heavy skillet, brown ham over medium-high heat in butter on both sides until heated through. Move ham to one side of the skillet; brown potatoes in drippings until tender. Sprinkle potatoes with parsley.
1 SERVING: 261 cal., 9g fat (5g sat. fat), 64mg chol., 1337mg sod., 21g carb. (1g sugars, 1g fiber), 28g pro.

EASY GLAZED SALMON

It only takes a handful of ingredients to make this delightful main dish.
I like this entree because of its simplicity—and yet it is so tasty!
—Tara Ernspiker, Falling Waters, WV

- -

TAKES: 25 min. • **MAKES:** 4 servings

⅓ cup packed brown sugar
¼ cup unsweetened pineapple juice
2 Tbsp. soy sauce
4 salmon fillets (6 oz. each)

1. Line a 15x10x1-in. baking pan with foil; grease the foil. Set aside. In a small bowl, combine the brown sugar, pineapple juice and soy sauce. Place salmon skin side down on prepared pan. Spoon sauce mixture over fish.
2. Bake, uncovered, at 350° for 20-25 minutes or until fish flakes easily with a fork, basting frequently with pan juices.
1 FILLET: 394 cal., 18g fat (4g sat. fat), 100mg chol., 568mg sod., 20g carb. (19g sugars, 0 fiber), 35g pro.

INSPIRED BY:
HARD ROCK CAFE'S
GRILLED NORWEGIAN SALMON

FANTASTIC FISH TACOS

This lighter alternative to traditional fried fish tacos is a hit with friends and family. Enjoy the crispy, crunchy entree at home tonight!
—Jennifer Palmer, Rancho Cucamonga, CA

INSPIRED BY:
CALIFORNIA PIZZA KITCHEN'S
CRISPY FISH TACOS

TAKES: 30 min. • **MAKES:** 4 servings

- ½ cup fat-free mayonnaise
- 1 Tbsp. lime juice
- 2 tsp. fat-free milk
- 1 large egg
- 1 tsp. water
- ⅓ cup dry bread crumbs
- 2 Tbsp. salt-free lemon-pepper seasoning
- 1 lb. mahi mahi or cod fillets, cut into 1-in. strips
- 4 corn tortillas (6 in.), warmed

TOPPINGS
- 1 cup coleslaw mix
- 2 medium tomatoes, chopped
- 1 cup shredded reduced-fat Mexican cheese blend
- 1 Tbsp. minced fresh cilantro

1. For sauce, in a small bowl, mix mayonnaise, lime juice and milk; refrigerate until serving.

2. In a shallow bowl, whisk together egg and water. In another bowl, toss bread crumbs with lemon pepper. Dip fish in egg mixture, then in crumb mixture, patting to help coating adhere.

3. Place a large nonstick skillet over medium-high heat. Add fish; cook 2-4 minutes per side or until golden brown and fish just begins to flake easily with a fork. Serve in tortillas with toppings and sauce.

1 TACO: 321 cal., 10g fat (5g sat. fat), 148mg chol., 632mg sod., 29g carb. (5g sugars, 4g fiber), 34g pro.
DIABETIC EXCHANGES: 4 lean meat, 2 starch.

HAVE IT YOUR WAY
Replace the lemon pepper with a dash of chili powder or cayenne pepper if you'd like to spice things up.

CRISPY ORANGE CHICKEN

We enjoy these tangy Asian-inspired nuggets in so many ways—over noodles or rice, in sandwiches and even on top of lettuce and cabbage.
—Darlene Brenden, Salem, OR

- -

TAKES: 30 min. • **MAKES:** 4 servings

- 16 oz. frozen popcorn chicken (about 4 cups)
- 1 Tbsp. canola oil
- 2 medium carrots, thinly sliced
- 1 garlic clove, minced
- 1½ tsp. grated orange zest
- 1 cup orange juice
- ⅓ cup hoisin sauce
- 3 Tbsp. sugar
- ¼ tsp. salt
- ¼ tsp. pepper
  Dash cayenne pepper
  Hot cooked rice

1. Bake popcorn chicken according to package directions.

2. Meanwhile, in a large skillet, heat oil over medium-high heat. Add carrots; cook and stir 3-5 minutes or until tender. Add minced garlic; cook 1 minute longer. Stir in orange zest, juice, hoisin sauce, sugar and seasonings; bring to a boil. Reduce heat; simmer, uncovered, 4-6 minutes or until thickened, stirring constantly.

3. Add chicken to skillet; toss to coat. Serve with rice.

1 CUP: 450 cal., 20g fat (3g sat. fat), 35mg chol., 1294mg sod., 56g carb. (25g sugars, 3g fiber), 14g pro.

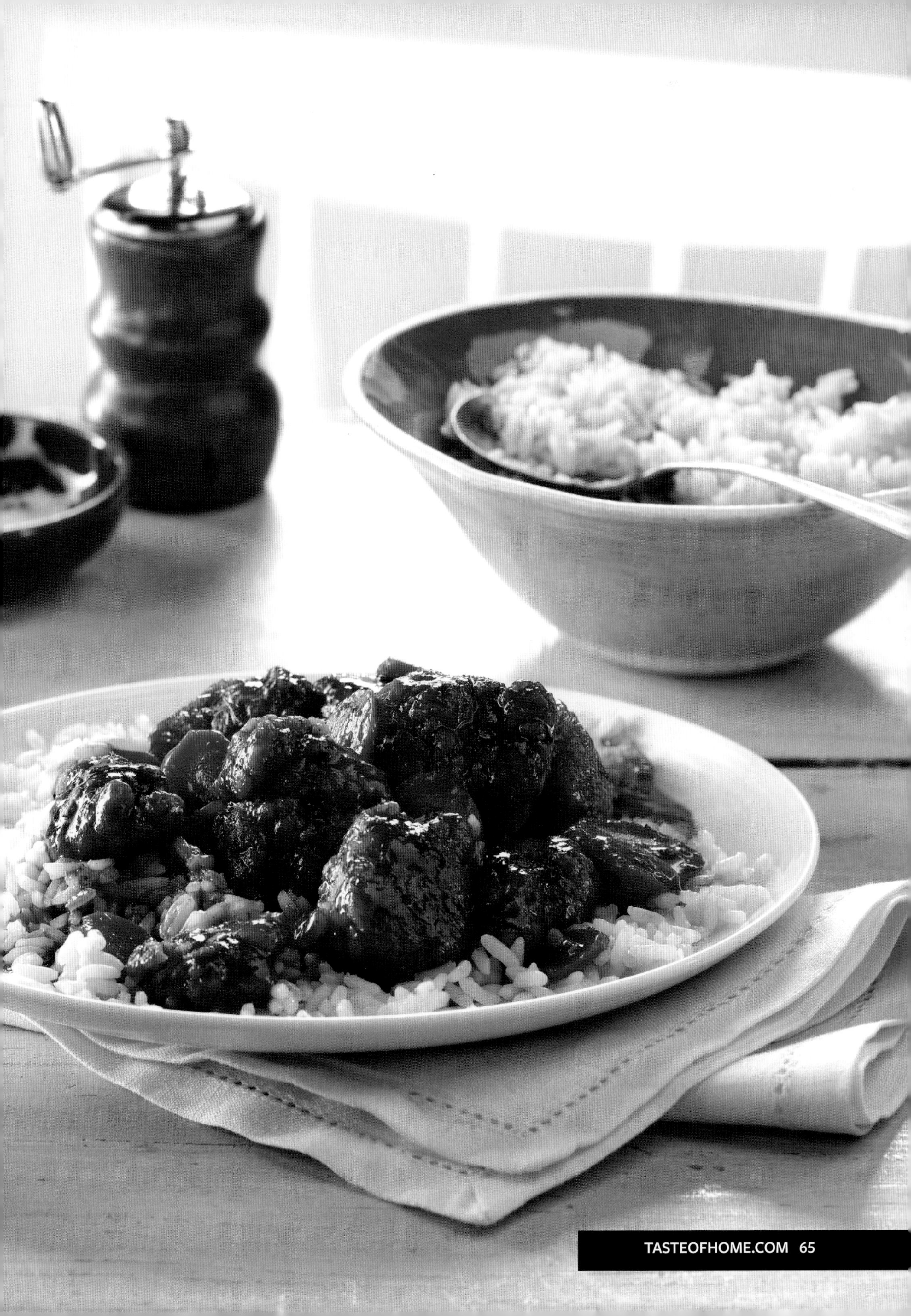

QUICK CHICKEN & DUMPLINGS

Oh, the things you can make with frozen biscuit dough! I like to use buttermilk biscuits to create this easy dumpling dish.
—Lakeya Astwood, Schenectady, NY

TAKES: 30 min. • **MAKES:** 6 servings

- 6 individually frozen biscuits
- ¼ cup chopped onion
- ¼ cup chopped green pepper
- 1 Tbsp. olive oil
- 4 cups shredded rotisserie chicken
- 3 cans (14½ oz. each) reduced-sodium chicken broth
- 1 can (4 oz.) mushroom stems and pieces, drained
- 1 tsp. chicken bouillon granules
- 1 tsp. minced fresh parsley
- ½ tsp. dried sage leaves
- ¼ tsp. dried rosemary, crushed
- ¼ tsp. pepper

1. Cut each biscuit into fourths; set aside. In a large saucepan, saute onion and green pepper in oil until tender. Stir in the chicken, broth, mushrooms, bouillon granules, parsley, sage, rosemary and pepper.
2. Bring to a boil. Reduce heat; add biscuits for dumplings. Cover and simmer until a toothpick inserted in the center of a dumpling comes out clean (do not lift cover while simmering), about 10 minutes.
1½ CUPS: 420 cal., 20g fat (5g sat. fat), 83mg chol., 1443mg sod., 26g carb. (6g sugars, 1g fiber), 34g pro.

WISCONSIN BUTTER-BASTED BURGERS

It's no secret Wisconsinites love their dairy—in fact, they love it so much they top their burgers with a generous pat of butter. My recipe is a lot like the butter burgers you'll find in popular restaurants all over the state.
—Becky Carver, North Royalton, OH

- -

TAKES: 30 min. • **MAKES:** 4 servings

1   lb. lean ground beef (90% lean)
½   tsp. seasoned salt
½   tsp. pepper
½   lb. fresh mushrooms
2   Tbsp. plus 4 tsp. butter, divided
4   hamburger buns, split
    Optional toppings: Tomato slices, lettuce leaves, dill pickle slices, ketchup and mustard

1. Sprinkle ground beef with seasoned salt and pepper. Pulse mushrooms in a food processor until finely chopped. Add to seasoned beef, mixing lightly but thoroughly. Shape into four ½-in.-thick patties.
2. In a large skillet, heat 2 Tbsp. butter over medium heat. Add burgers; cook 6-8 minutes on each side, basting with butter, until a thermometer reads 160°. Remove from heat; keep warm. Add bun tops to skillet; toast until golden brown.
3. Transfer burgers to bun bottoms. Top each with 1 tsp. butter. Replace bun tops. Serve with toppings if desired.
1 BURGER: 400 cal., 21g fat (10g sat. fat), 96mg chol., 543mg sod., 24g carb. (3g sugars, 1g fiber), 28g pro.

BANDITO CHILI DOGS

These deluxe chili dogs are a surefire hit at family functions. Adults and children alike love the cheesy chili sauce, and the toppings are fun!
—Marion Lowery, Medford, OR

PREP: 15 min. • **COOK:** 4 hours • **MAKES:** 10 servings

- 1 pkg. (1 lb.) hot dogs
- 2 cans (15 oz. each) chili without beans
- 1 can (10¾ oz.) condensed cheddar cheese soup, undiluted
- 1 can (4 oz.) chopped green chiles
- 10 hot dog buns, split
- 1 medium onion, chopped
- 1 to 2 cups corn chips, coarsely crushed
- 1 cup shredded cheddar cheese

1. Place hot dogs in a 3-qt. slow cooker. In a large bowl, combine the chili, soup and green chiles; pour over hot dogs. Cover and cook on low for 4-5 hours.

2. Serve hot dogs in buns; top with chili mixture, chopped onion, corn chips and cheese.

1 CHILI DOG: 450 cal., 23g fat (10g sat. fat), 53mg chol., 1442mg sod., 43g carb. (6g sugars, 3g fiber), 19g pro.

INSPIRED BY:
PORTILLO'S
CHILI CHEESE DOG

Popular Pizza & Pasta

FRIDAY NIGHT CALLS FOR PIZZA & PASTA! HANG UP THE PHONE: THESE HEARTWARMING ITALIAN FAVES ARE BETTER THAN TAKEOUT.

**BARBECUED CHICKEN
PIZZAS, P. 81**
INSPIRED BY:
UNO PIZZERIA & GRILL'S
BBQ CHICKEN PIZZA

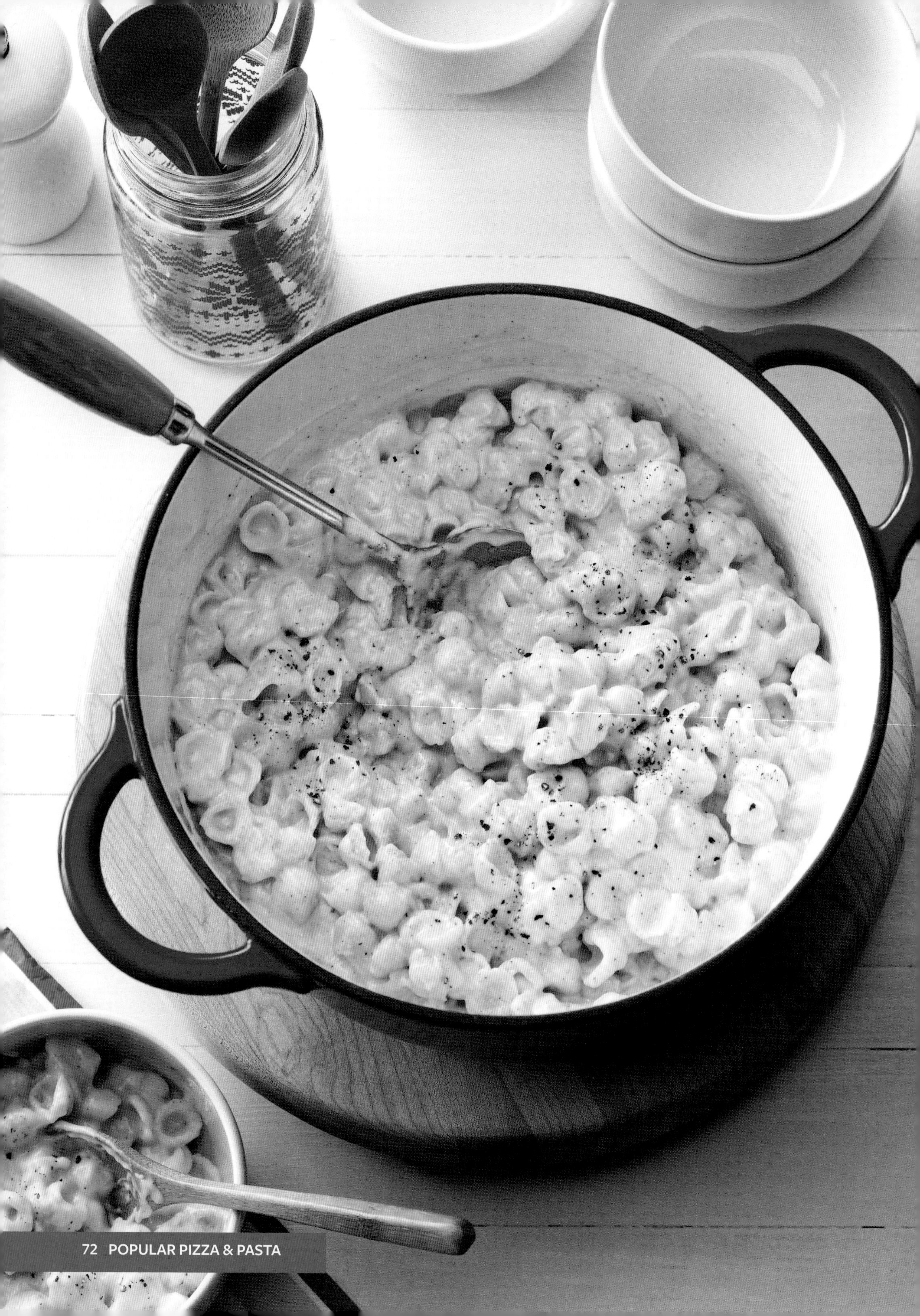

WHITE CHEDDAR MAC & CHEESE

My mac and cheese is simple and has lots of flavor from the cheeses and ground chipotle chile. I use conchiglie pasta because its large openings allow more yummy melted cheese to pool inside.
—Colleen Delawder, Herndon, VA

INSPIRED BY:
PANERA BREAD'S
MAC & CHEESE

- -

TAKES: 25 min. • **MAKES:** 8 servings

- 1 pkg. (16 oz.) small pasta shells
- ½ cup butter, cubed
- ½ cup all-purpose flour
- ½ tsp. onion powder
- ½ tsp. ground chipotle pepper
- ½ tsp. pepper
- ¼ tsp. salt
- 4 cups 2% milk
- 2 cups shredded sharp white cheddar cheese
- 2 cups shredded Manchego or additional white cheddar cheese

1. In a 6-qt. stockpot, cook pasta according to package directions. Drain; return to pot.

2. Meanwhile, in a large saucepan, melt butter over medium heat. Stir in flour and seasonings until smooth; gradually whisk in milk. Bring to a boil, stirring constantly; cook and stir until thickened, 6-8 minutes. Remove from heat; stir in the cheeses until melted. Add to pasta; toss to coat.

1 CUP: 650 cal., 35g fat (22g sat. fat), 101mg chol., 607mg sod., 55g carb. (8g sugars, 2g fiber), 27g pro.

INSPIRED BY:
CALIFORNIA PIZZA KITCHEN'S
HAWAIIAN PIZZA

BIG KAHUNA PIZZA

A prebaked pizza crust and refrigerated barbecued pork make this tasty supper idea super fast and super easy. Cut into bite-sized pieces, it can double as a great last-minute appetizer, too.

—Joni Hilton, Rocklin, CA

- -

TAKES: 30 min. • **MAKES:** 6 servings

- 1   prebaked 12-in. pizza crust
- 1   carton (16 oz.) refrigerated fully cooked barbecued shredded pork
- 1   can (20 oz.) pineapple chunks, drained
- ⅓   cup chopped red onion
- 2   cups shredded part-skim mozzarella cheese

1. Place pizza crust on an ungreased 12-in. pizza pan. Spread shredded pork over the crust; top with pineapple and onion. Sprinkle with cheese.
2. Bake at 350° for 20-25 minutes or until cheese is melted.
1 SLICE: 443 cal., 12g fat (5g sat. fat), 45mg chol., 1133mg sod., 56g carb. (25g sugars, 2g fiber), 27g pro.

CHICKEN PESTO WITH PASTA

Keep a container of pesto in the freezer. The next time you have leftover chicken, whip up this simple pasta for lunch or dinner.
—*Taste of Home* Test Kitchen

INSPIRED BY:
NOODLES & COMPANY'S
PESTO CAVATAPPI

TAKES: 20 min. • **MAKES:** 8 servings

- 1 pkg. (16 oz.) cellentani or spiral pasta
- 2 cups cubed rotisserie chicken
- 2 medium tomatoes, chopped
- 1 container (7 oz.) prepared pesto
- ¼ cup pine nuts, toasted

In a Dutch oven, cook pasta according to package directions; drain and return to pan. Stir in chicken, tomatoes and pesto; heat through. Sprinkle with pine nuts.

NOTE: To toast nuts, bake in a shallow pan in a 350° oven for 5-10 minutes or cook in a skillet over low heat until lightly browned, stirring occasionally.

1¼ CUPS: 404 cal., 16g fat (3g sat. fat), 31mg chol., 348mg sod., 46g carb. (4g sugars, 3g fiber), 20g pro.

PEPPERONI PAN PIZZA

I've spent years trying to come up with the perfect pizza crust and sauce, and they're paired up in this recipe. I fix this pizza for my family often, and it really satisfies my husband and three sons.

—Susan Lindahl, Alford, FL

- -

PREP: 30 min. • **BAKE:** 10 min. • **MAKES:** 2 pizzas (4 servings each)

2¾ to 3 cups all-purpose flour
1 pkg. (¼ oz.) active dry yeast
¼ tsp. salt
1 cup warm water (120° to 130°)
1 Tbsp. canola oil

SAUCE
1 can (14½ oz.) diced tomatoes, undrained
1 can (6 oz.) tomato paste
1 Tbsp. canola oil
1 tsp. salt
½ tsp. each dried basil, oregano, marjoram and thyme
¼ tsp. garlic powder
¼ tsp. pepper

PIZZAS
1 pkg. (3½ oz.) sliced pepperoni
5 cups shredded part-skim mozzarella cheese
¼ cup grated Parmesan cheese
¼ cup grated Romano cheese

1. In a large bowl, combine 2 cups flour, yeast and salt. Add water and oil; beat until smooth. Add enough remaining flour to form a soft dough.

2. Turn onto a floured surface; knead until smooth and elastic, 5-7 minutes. Cover and let stand for 10 minutes. Meanwhile, in a small bowl, combine tomatoes, tomato paste, oil and seasonings.

3. Divide dough in half; press into two 15x10x1-in. baking pans coated with cooking spray. Prick dough generously with a fork. Bake crusts at 425° until lightly browned,12-16 minutes.

4. Spread sauce over crusts; top with pepperoni and cheeses. Bake until the cheese is melted, 8-10 minutes. Cut into squares.

FREEZE OPTION: Bake crusts and assemble pizzas as directed. Securely wrap and freeze unbaked pizzas. To use, unwrap pizzas; bake as directed, increasing time as necessary.

1 SERVING: 431 cal., 20g fat (10g sat. fat), 51mg chol., 985mg sod., 38g carb. (7g sugars, 3g fiber), 25g pro.

INSPIRED BY:
THE CHEESECAKE FACTORY'S
PASTA CARBONARA

QUICK CARBONARA

Carbonara is a dinnertime classic, but my version cuts down on the time it takes to make. Loaded with ham, bacon, garlic and Parmesan, it doesn't skimp on flavor. We add olives, but try peas if your family likes them.
—Carole Martin, Tallahassee, FL

- -

TAKES: 30 min. • **MAKES:** 6 servings

- 12   oz. uncooked spaghetti
- 3   Tbsp. butter
- 3   Tbsp. canola oil
- 2   garlic cloves, minced
- 3   cups cubed fully cooked ham
- 8   bacon strips, cooked and crumbled
- 2   Tbsp. minced fresh parsley
- ¾   cup sliced ripe or pimiento-stuffed olives
- ½   cup grated Parmesan cheese

1. Cook the spaghetti according to package directions; drain.

2. In a large skillet, heat butter and oil over medium heat; saute the garlic 1 minute. Stir in ham and bacon; heat through. Add spaghetti and parsley; toss to combine.

3. Remove from heat. Stir in olives and cheese.

1 SERVING: 513 cal., 24g fat (8g sat. fat), 73mg chol., 1333mg sod., 45g carb. (2g sugars, 2g fiber), 28g pro.

GARLICKY CHICKEN PIZZA

Tomatoes, olives and goat cheese really brighten up this white pizza. I like to cook extra chicken for this recipe while making another meal. Just make sure the tomatoes are well drained to keep the crust nice and crispy.
—Teri Otte, Cannon Falls, MN

- -

TAKES: 25 min. • **MAKES:** 6 servings

- 1 tube (13.8 oz.) refrigerated pizza crust
- 2 Tbsp. olive oil
- 2 garlic cloves, minced
- 1 can (14½ oz.) diced tomatoes, well drained
- 1 large onion, thinly sliced (about 1 cup)
- ⅓ cup pitted kalamata olives, halved
- 2 cups cubed or shredded cooked chicken
- 1⅓ cups crumbled goat cheese
- 1 tsp. minced fresh rosemary or ¼ tsp. dried rosemary, crushed
- ½ tsp. garlic salt
- ½ tsp. pepper

1. Preheat oven to 400°. Unroll and press dough onto bottom and ½ in. up sides of a greased 15x10x1-in. baking pan. Bake 8-10 minutes or until edges are lightly browned.

2. Mix oil and garlic; brush over crust. Top with tomatoes, onion, olives, chicken and goat cheese. Sprinkle with rosemary, garlic salt and pepper. Bake 10-12 minutes or until crust is golden.

1 PIECE: 418 cal., 19g fat (6g sat. fat), 73mg chol., 957mg sod., 39g carb. (7g sugars, 3g fiber), 25g pro.

BARBECUED CHICKEN PIZZAS

So fast and so easy with refrigerated pizza crust, these saucy, smoky pizzas make quick fans with their hot-off-the-grill, rustic flavor. They're perfect for spur-of-the-moment cookouts and summer dinners on the patio.

—Alicia Trevithick, Temecula, CA

- -

PREP: 25 min. • **GRILL:** 10 min. • **MAKES:** 2 pizzas (4 pieces each)

- 2 boneless skinless chicken breast halves (6 oz. each)
- ¼ tsp. pepper
- 1 cup barbecue sauce, divided
- 1 tube (13.8 oz.) refrigerated pizza crust
- 2 tsp. olive oil
- 2 cups shredded Gouda cheese
- 1 small red onion, halved and thinly sliced
- ¼ cup minced fresh cilantro

1. Sprinkle the chicken breasts with pepper; place on an oiled grill rack over medium heat. Grill, covered, until a thermometer reads 165°, 5-7 minutes per side, basting frequently with ½ cup barbecue sauce during the last 4 minutes. Cool slightly. Cut into cubes.

2. Divide dough in half. On a well-greased large sheet of heavy-duty foil, press each portion of dough into a 10x8-in. rectangle; brush lightly with oil. Invert dough onto the grill rack; peel off the foil. Grill, covered, over medium heat until bottom is lightly browned, 1-2 minutes.

3. Remove from grill. Spread grilled sides with remaining barbecue sauce. Top with cheese, chicken and onion. Grill, covered, until bottom is lightly browned and cheese is melted, 2-3 minutes. Sprinkle pizzas with cilantro.

1 PIECE: 339 cal., 12g fat (6g sat. fat), 56mg chol., 956mg sod., 39g carb. (15g sugars, 1g fiber), 20g pro.

MEAT SAUCE FOR SPAGHETTI

Here's a hearty meat sauce that turns ordinary spaghetti and garlic bread into a feast. If you don't have spaghetti noodles, no problem! I've successfully swirled and served up this sauce with nearly every pasta shape in my pantry.
—Mary Tallman, Arbor Vitae, WI

PREP: 30 min. • **COOK:** 8 hours • **MAKES:** 9 servings

1	lb. ground beef
1	lb. bulk Italian sausage
1	can (28 oz.) crushed tomatoes, undrained
1	medium green pepper, chopped
1	medium onion, chopped
2	medium carrots, finely chopped
1	cup water
1	can (8 oz.) tomato sauce
1	can (6 oz.) tomato paste
1	Tbsp. brown sugar
1	Tbsp. Italian seasoning
2	garlic cloves, minced
½	tsp. salt
¼	tsp. pepper
	Hot cooked spaghetti

1. In a large skillet, cook beef and sausage over medium heat until no longer pink; drain.
2. Transfer to a 5-qt. slow cooker. Stir in the tomatoes, green pepper, onion, carrots, water, tomato sauce, tomato paste, brown sugar, Italian seasoning, garlic, salt and pepper. Cover and cook on low for 8-10 hours or until bubbly. Serve with spaghetti.
FREEZE OPTION: Do not cook spaghetti. Freeze cooled meat sauce in freezer containers. To use, partially thaw in refrigerator overnight. Cook spaghetti according to package directions. Place sauce in a large skillet; heat through, stirring occasionally and adding a little water if necessary. Serve over spaghetti.
1 CUP: 286 cal., 17g fat (6g sat. fat), 58mg chol., 767mg sod., 17g carb. (9g sugars, 4g fiber), 18g pro.

Favorite Odds & Ends

FROM SHAKES AND FRIES TO BREADS AND SIDES, THESE DOUBLE-TAKE RECIPES ROUND OUT HOMEMADE MENUS WITH FAMILIAR FLAIR.

THIN MINT MILK SHAKE, P. 96
INSPIRED BY: MCDONALD'S
SHAMROCK SHAKE

CHEESE FRIES

I came up with this recipe after my daughter had cheese fries at a restaurant and couldn't stop talking about them. She loves that I can fix them so quickly at home.
—Melissa Tatum, Greensboro, NC

INSPIRED BY:
SHAKE SHACK'S
CHEESE FRIES

- -

TAKES: 20 min. • **MAKES:** 8 servings

- 1   pkg. (28 oz.) frozen steak fries
- 1   can (10¾ oz.) condensed cheddar cheese soup, undiluted
- ¼   cup 2% milk
- ½   tsp. garlic powder
- ¼   tsp. onion powder
-     Paprika

1. Arrange the steak fries in a single layer in 2 greased 15x10x1-in. baking pans. Bake at 450° for 15-18 minutes or until fries are tender and golden brown.

2. Meanwhile, in a small saucepan, combine the soup, milk, garlic powder and onion powder; heat through. Drizzle over fries; sprinkle with paprika.

1 SERVING: 166 cal., 5g fat (2g sat. fat), 2mg chol., 657mg sod., 27g carb. (3g sugars, 3g fiber), 3g pro.

INSPIRED BY:
PANDA EXPRESS'
FRIED RICE

SUPER QUICK CHICKEN FRIED RICE

After my first child was born, I needed meals that were satisfying and fast. This fried rice is now part of our regular dinner rotation.
—Alicia Gower, Auburn, NY

TAKES: 30 min. • **MAKES:** 6 servings

- 1 pkg. (12 oz.) frozen mixed vegetables
- 2 Tbsp. olive oil, divided
- 2 large eggs, lightly beaten
- 4 Tbsp. sesame oil, divided
- 3 pkg. (8.8 oz. each) ready-to-serve garden vegetable rice
- 1 rotisserie chicken, skin removed, shredded
- ¼ tsp. salt
- ¼ tsp. pepper

1. Prepare frozen vegetables according to package directions. Meanwhile, in a large skillet, heat 1 Tbsp. olive oil over medium-high heat. Pour in eggs; cook and stir until eggs are thickened and no liquid egg remains. Remove from pan.
2. In same skillet, heat 2 Tbsp. sesame oil and remaining olive oil over medium-high heat. Add rice; cook and stir until rice begins to brown, 10-12 minutes.
3. Stir in chicken, salt and pepper. Add eggs and vegetables; heat through, breaking eggs into small pieces and stirring to combine. Drizzle with the remaining sesame oil.
1½ CUPS: 548 cal., 25g fat (5g sat. fat), 163mg chol., 934mg sod., 43g carb. (3g sugars, 3g fiber), 38g pro.

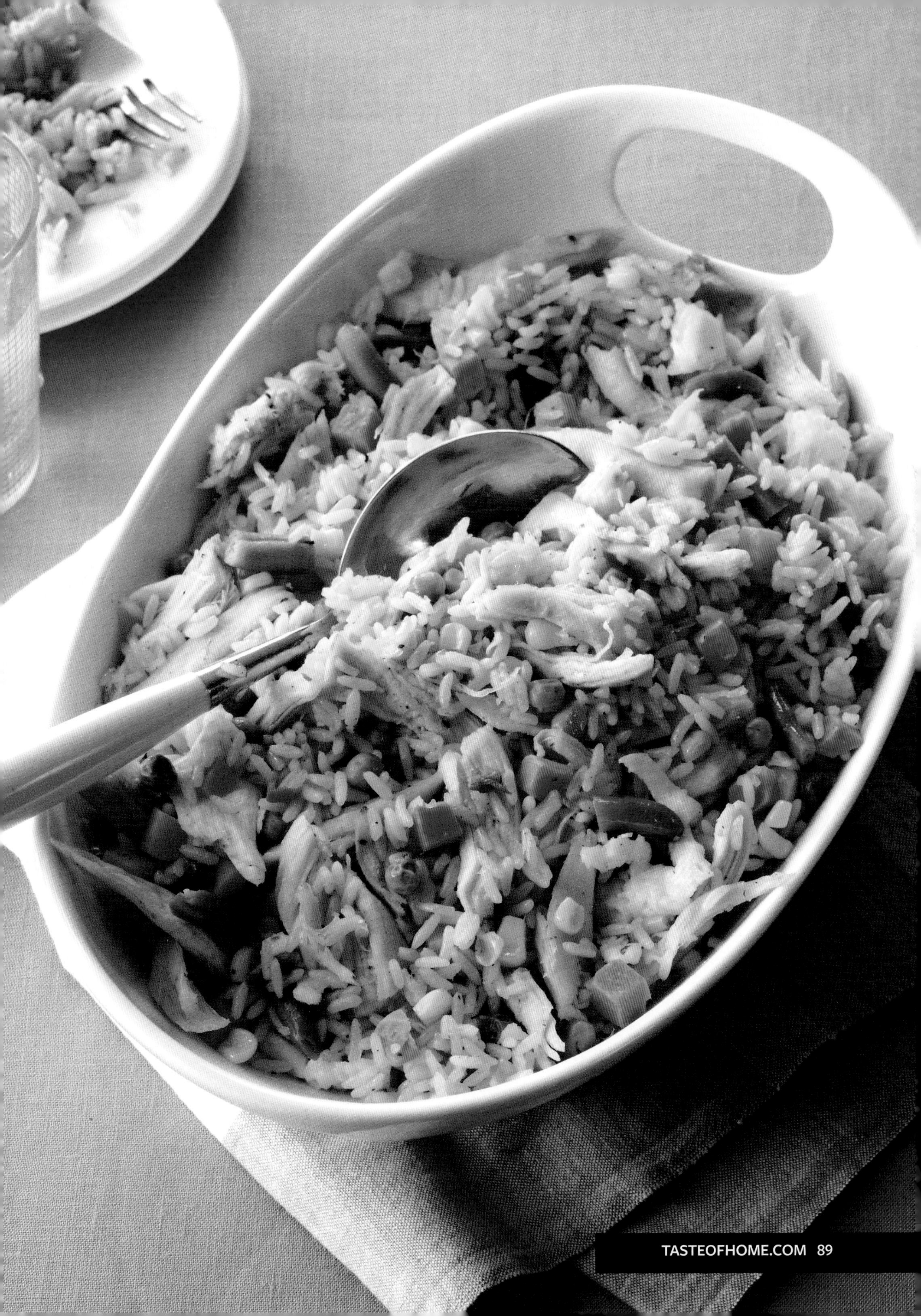

DELUXE MASHED POTATOES

When it comes to mashed potatoes, this version is one of my favorites. I can make the potatoes ahead, set them in the refrigerator and pop them into the oven just prior to dinnertime. When my grandchildren come visit, I have to double the recipe!
—Vivian Bailey, Cedar Falls, IA

PREP: 30 min. • **BAKE:** 35 min. • **MAKES:** 6 servings

4	to 5 large potatoes (about 2½ lbs.)
3	oz. cream cheese, softened
½	cup sour cream
1	Tbsp. chopped chives
¾	tsp. onion salt
¼	tsp. pepper
1	Tbsp. butter
	Paprika, optional

Peel and cube the potatoes; place in a saucepan and cover with water. Cook over medium heat until tender; drain. Mash until smooth (do not add milk or butter). Stir in cream cheese, sour cream, chives, onion salt and pepper. Spoon into a greased 1½-qt. baking dish. Dot with butter; sprinkle with paprika if desired. Cover and bake at 350° for 35-40 minutes or until the potatoes are heated through.

¾ CUP: 301 cal., 10g fat (7g sat. fat), 34mg chol., 313mg sod., 45g carb. (5g sugars, 4g fiber), 7g pro.

SAVORY BISCUIT-BREADSTICKS

I love to experiment in the kitchen with simple ingredients such as refrigerated biscuits. The results usually are a big hit, and these super fast breadsticks are no exception.
—Billy Hensley, Mount Carmel, TN

- -

TAKES: 20 min. • **MAKES:** 10 breadsticks

- ½ cup grated Parmesan cheese
- 2 tsp. dried minced garlic
- ¼ tsp. crushed red pepper flakes
- 1 tube (12 oz.) refrigerated buttermilk biscuits
- 2 Tbsp. olive oil

Preheat oven to 400°. In a shallow bowl, mix cheese, garlic and pepper flakes. Roll each biscuit into a 6-in. rope. Brush lightly with oil; roll in the cheese mixture. Place on a greased baking sheet. Bake until golden brown, 8-10 minutes.

1 BREADSTICK: 142 cal., 8g fat (2g sat. fat), 3mg chol., 353mg sod., 16g carb. (2g sugars, 0 fiber), 3g pro.

INSPIRED BY:
OLIVE GARDEN'S BREADSTICKS

HAVE IT YOUR WAY
Not a fan of red pepper flakes? Feel free to take them out or replace them with Italian seasoning.

SWEET RASPBERRY TEA

You only need a handful of ingredients to stir together this bright and refreshing sipper as the weather heats up.

—*Taste of Home* Test Kitchen

INSPIRED BY:
RUBY TUESDAY'S
RASPBERRY ICED TEA

PREP: 10 min. • **COOK:** 15 min. + chilling • **MAKES:** 15 servings

- 4 qt. water, divided
- 10 tea bags
- 1 pkg. (12 oz.) frozen unsweetened raspberries, thawed and undrained
- 1 cup sugar
- 3 Tbsp. lime juice

1. In a saucepan, bring 2 qt. water to a boil; remove from heat. Add tea bags; steep, covered, 5-8 minutes according to taste. Discard tea bags.
2. Place raspberries, sugar and remaining water in a large saucepan; bring to a boil, stirring to dissolve the sugar. Reduce heat; simmer, uncovered, 3 minutes. Press mixture through a fine-mesh strainer into a bowl; discard pulp and seeds.
3. In a large pitcher, combine tea, raspberry syrup and lime juice. Refrigerate, covered, until cold.

1 CUP: 63 cal., 0 fat (0 sat. fat), 0 chol., 0 sod., 16g carb. (15g sugars, 1g fiber), 0 pro.

BUTTERY CORNBREAD

A friend gave me this recipe several years ago, and it's my favorite. I love to serve the melt-in-your-mouth cornbread hot from the oven with butter and syrup. It gets rave reviews on holidays and at potluck dinners.
—Nicole Callen, Auburn, CA

- -

PREP: 15 min. • **BAKE:** 25 min. • **MAKES:** 15 servings

- ⅔ cup butter, softened
- 1 cup sugar
- 3 large eggs, room temperature
- 1⅔ cups 2% milk
- 2⅓ cups all-purpose flour
- 1 cup cornmeal
- 4½ tsp. baking powder
- 1 tsp. salt

1. Preheat oven to 400°. In a large bowl, cream butter and sugar until light and fluffy. Combine eggs and milk. Combine flour, cornmeal, baking powder and salt; add to creamed mixture alternately with egg mixture.
2. Pour into a greased 13x9-in. baking pan. Bake 22-27 minutes or until a toothpick inserted in center comes out clean. Cut into squares; serve warm.
1 PIECE: 259 cal., 10g fat (6g sat. fat), 68mg chol., 386mg sod., 37g carb. (15g sugars, 1g fiber), 5g pro.

INSPIRED BY:
MCDONALD'S
SHAMROCK SHAKE

THIN MINT MILK SHAKE

Save a sleeve of those yummy chocolate-mint Girl Scout cookies to use for creamy milk shakes. They go over big with kids and adults alike.
—Shauna Sever, San Francisco, CA

- -

TAKES: 5 min. • **MAKES:** 2 servings

  3 2% milk plus a dash of peppermint extract
1¼ to 1½ cups vanilla ice cream
  7 Girl Scout Thin Mint cookies
     Green food coloring

Place all ingredients in a blender in order listed; cover and process until blended. Serve immediately.
⅔ **CUP:** 363 cal., 12g fat (7g sat. fat), 36mg chol., 70mg sod., 49g carb. (47g sugars, 1g fiber), 3g pro.

CHEDDAR BISCUITS

These biscuits have a cheesy richness that everyone will love. I like to serve them with steaming bowls of chili or hearty beef soup.
—Alicia Rooker, Milwaukee, WI

- -

TAKES: 30 min. • **MAKES:** 15 biscuits

1	cup all-purpose flour
1	cup cake flour
1½	tsp. baking powder
¾	tsp. salt
½	tsp. garlic powder, divided
¼	tsp. baking soda
4	Tbsp. cold butter, divided
⅓	cup finely shredded cheddar cheese
1	cup buttermilk
½	tsp. dried parsley flakes

1. In a large bowl, combine the flours, baking powder, salt, ¼ tsp. garlic powder and baking soda. Cut in 3 Tbsp. butter until mixture resembles coarse crumbs; add cheese. Stir in buttermilk just until moistened.

2. Drop by 2 tablespoonfuls 2 in. apart onto baking sheets coated with cooking spray. Bake at 425° for 10-12 minutes or until golden brown. Melt remaining butter; stir in parsley and remaining garlic powder. Brush over biscuits. Serve warm.

1 BISCUIT: 106 cal., 4g fat (3g sat. fat), 11mg chol., 233mg sod., 14g carb. (1g sugars, 0 fiber), 3g pro.

INSPIRED BY:
RED LOBSTER'S
CHEDDAR BAY BISCUITS

Double-Take Desserts

IS THE BEST PART OF DINNER THE DESSERT? IT JUST MIGHT BE! NOW YOU CAN HAVE ALL THE PLEASURE OF YOUR FAVORITE INDULGENT RESTAURANT DESSERT WITHOUT LEAVING HOME!

DULCE DE LECHE CHEESECAKE
P. 107
INSPIRED BY: THE CHEESECAKE FACTORY'S
DULCE DE LECHE CARAMEL CHEESECAKE

OLD-TIME CUSTARD ICE CREAM

My most memorable summertime dessert for get-togethers has always been homemade ice cream. This recipe is so rich and creamy... it's the perfect splurge on a hot summer afternoon.
—Martha Self, Montgomery, TX

INSPIRED BY:
CULVER'S
VANILLA FROZEN CUSTARD

PREP: 55 min. + chilling • **PROCESS:** 55 min./batch + freezing
MAKES: 2¾ qt.

- 1½ cups sugar
- ¼ cup all-purpose flour
- ½ tsp. salt
- 4 cups whole milk
- 4 large eggs, lightly beaten
- 2 pints heavy whipping cream
- 3 Tbsp. vanilla extract

1. In a large heavy saucepan, combine sugar, flour and salt. Gradually add milk until smooth. Cook and stir over medium heat until thickened and bubbly. Reduce heat to low; cook and stir 2 minutes longer. Remove from heat.

2. In a small bowl, whisk a small amount of the hot mixture into eggs; return all to pan, whisking constantly. Bring to a gentle boil; cook and stir 2 minutes. Remove from heat immediately.

3. Quickly transfer to a large bowl; place bowl in a pan of ice water. Stir gently and occasionally for 2 minutes. Press plastic wrap onto the surface of the custard. Refrigerate for several hours or overnight.

4. Stir cream and vanilla into the custard. Fill the cylinder of an ice cream freezer two-thirds full; freeze according to manufacturer's directions. (Refrigerate the remaining mixture until ready to freeze.) Transfer ice cream to freezer containers, allowing headspace for expansion. Freeze for 2-4 hours or until firm. Repeat with remaining ice cream mixture.

½ CUP: 252 cal., 18g fat (11g sat. fat), 88mg chol., 98mg sod., 18g carb. (17g sugars, 0 fiber), 4g pro.

SANDY'S CHOCOLATE CAKE

Whenever anyone tastes this cake, they say it's the best chocolate cake ever. Velvety, rich and delicious, it bakes up high. Assembled in layers with a rich frosting, it's a luscious tower of chocolate.
—Sandy Johnson, Tioga, PA

PREP: 30 min. • **BAKE:** 30 min. + cooling • **MAKES:** 16 servings

  1 cup butter, softened
  3 cups packed brown sugar
  4 large eggs, room temperature
  2 tsp. vanilla extract
  2⅔ cups all-purpose flour
  ¾ cup baking cocoa
  3 tsp. baking soda
  ½ tsp. salt
  1⅓ cups sour cream
  1⅓ cups boiling water

FROSTING
  ½ cup butter, cubed
  3 oz. unsweetened chocolate, chopped
  3 oz. semisweet chocolate, chopped
  5 cups confectioners' sugar
  1 cup sour cream
  2 tsp. vanilla extract

1. Preheat oven to 350°. Grease and flour three 9-in. round baking pans; set aside.

2. In a large bowl, cream butter and brown sugar until light and fluffy. Add eggs, 1 at a time, beating well after each addition. Beat in vanilla. In another bowl, whisk flour, cocoa, baking soda and salt; add to the creamed mixture alternately with sour cream, beating well after each addition. Stir in water until blended. Transfer to prepared pans. Bake until a toothpick comes out clean, 30-35 minutes. Cool in pans 10 minutes; remove to wire racks to cool completely.

3. For frosting, in a metal bowl over simmering water, melt butter and chocolates; stir until smooth. Cool slightly.

4. In a large bowl, combine confectioners' sugar, sour cream and vanilla. Add the chocolate mixture; beat until smooth. Spread frosting between the layers and over the top and sides of cake. Refrigerate leftovers.

1 SLICE: 685 cal., 29g fat (18g sat. fat), 115mg chol., 505mg sod., 102g carb. (81g sugars, 3g fiber), 7g pro.

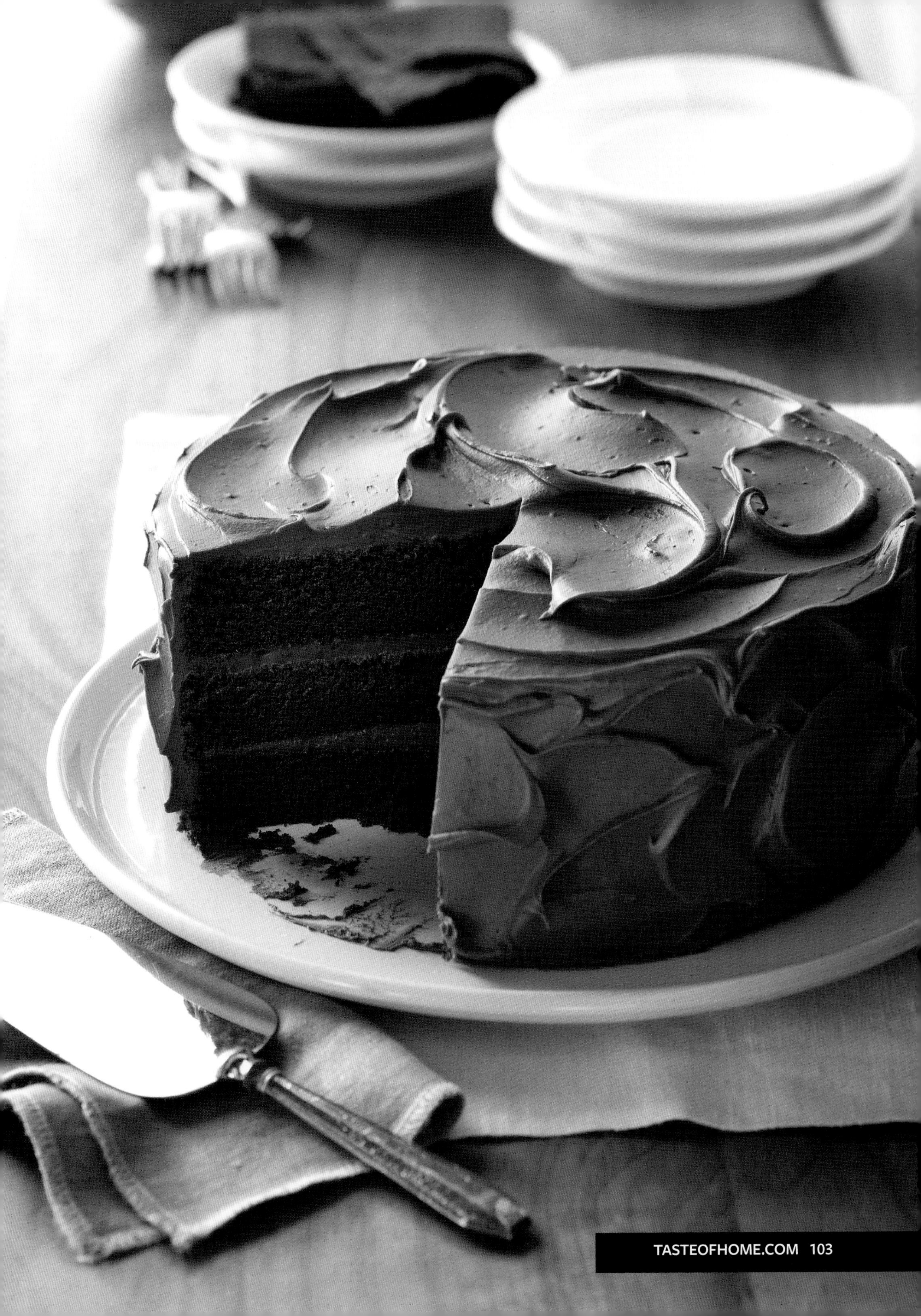

WINNING APPLE CRISP

I live in apple country, and there's nothing better than an old-fashioned apple crisp. Sweet-tart apples topped with a crunchy spiced topping—and finished off with with a scoop of vanilla ice cream. Dessert perfection!
—Gertrude Bartnick, Portage, WI

- -

PREP: 20 min. • **BAKE:** 1 hour • **MAKES:** 8 servings

1   cup all-purpose flour
¾   cup rolled oats
1   cup packed brown sugar
1   tsp. ground cinnamon
½   cup butter, softened
4   cups chopped peeled apples
1   cup sugar
2   Tbsp. cornstarch
1   cup water
1   tsp. vanilla extract
        Vanilla ice cream, optional

1. Preheat oven to 350°. In a large bowl, combine the first 4 ingredients. Cut in butter until crumbly. Press half into a greased 2½-qt. baking dish or a 9-in. square baking pan. Cover with apples.
2. In a small saucepan, combine the sugar, cornstarch, water and vanilla. Bring to a boil; cook and stir 2 minutes or until thick and clear. Pour over the apples. Sprinkle with the remaining crumb mixture.
3. Bake for 60-65 minutes or until apples are tender. Serve warm, with ice cream if desired.
1 SERVING: 426 cal., 12g fat (7g sat. fat), 31mg chol., 127mg sod., 79g carb. (58g sugars, 2g fiber), 3g pro.
WINNING PEAR CRISP: Substitute pears for the apples.

WHITE CHOCOLATE PEPPERMINT CRUNCH

This is my favorite confection to make at Christmas. Not only is it easy, it's delicious as well. I like to fill small bags with the crunchy candy to place in gift baskets.
—Nancy Shelton, Boaz, KY

- -

PREP: 15 min. + chilling • **COOK:** 5 min. • **MAKES:** about 1½ lbs.

- 1 **lb. white candy coating, coarsely chopped**
- 1 **Tbsp. butter**
- 1 **Tbsp. canola oil**
- 1 **cup chopped peppermint candies or candy canes**

1. Line a baking sheet with parchment or waxed paper. In a microwave, melt candy coating; stir until smooth. Stir in butter and oil until blended. Stir in candies. Spread to desired thickness on prepared pan.
2. Refrigerate until firm. Break into pieces. Store candy in an airtight container in the refrigerator.
1 OZ.: 125 cal., 6g fat (5g sat. fat), 1mg chol., 5mg sod., 17g carb. (15g sugars, 0 fiber), 0 pro.

DULCE DE LECHE CHEESECAKE

If you can't find dulce de leche at your grocery store, try caramel ice cream topping instead. It tastes different, but this decadent dessert will still be amazing.
—Sonia Lipham, Ranburne, AL

INSPIRED BY:
THE CHEESECAKE FACTORY'S
DULCE DE LECHE CARAMEL CHEESECAKE

PREP: 40 min. • **BAKE:** 1 hour + chilling • **MAKES:** 16 servings

- 1¾ cups crushed gingersnap cookies (about 35 cookies)
- ¼ cup finely chopped walnuts
- 1 Tbsp. sugar
- ½ tsp. ground cinnamon
- 6 Tbsp. butter, melted

FILLING
- 3 pkg. (8 oz. each) cream cheese, softened
- 1 cup plus 2 Tbsp. sugar
- ¼ cup 2% milk
- 2 Tbsp. all-purpose flour
- 1 tsp. vanilla extract
- 3 large eggs, lightly beaten
- 1 can (13.4 oz.) dulce de leche

TOPPINGS
- 1 cup (6 oz.) semisweet chocolate chips
- 1½ tsp. chili powder
- ½ cup dulce de leche
- 3 Tbsp. hot water

1. Preheat oven to 350°. Place a greased 9-in. springform pan on a double thickness of heavy-duty foil (about 18 in. square). Securely wrap foil around pan. In a large bowl, combine cookie crumbs, walnuts, sugar, cinnamon and butter. Press onto the bottom and 2 in. up sides of the prepared pan.

2. In a large bowl, beat cream cheese and sugar until smooth. Beat in milk, flour and vanilla. Add eggs; beat on low speed just until combined. Pour into crust.

3. Pour dulce de leche into a microwave-safe bowl; microwave at 50% power until softened. Drop dulce de leche by tablespoonfuls over batter; cut through batter with a knife to swirl.

4. Place springform pan in a large baking pan; add 1 in. of hot water to larger pan. Bake for 60-70 minutes or until center is just set and the top appears dull.

5. Remove springform pan from water bath. Cool on a wire rack for 10 minutes. Carefully run a knife around edge of pan to loosen; cool for 1 hour.

6. In a microwave-safe bowl, melt chips; stir until smooth. Stir in chili powder. Spread over cheesecake. Refrigerate overnight. Remove sides of pan.

7. In a small bowl, whisk dulce de leche and hot water until smooth; drizzle over cheesecake.

NOTE: This recipe was tested with Nestle La Lechera dulce de leche; look for it in the international foods section. If using Eagle Brand dulce de leche (caramel-flavored sauce), thicken according to package directions before using.

1 SLICE: 468 cal., 28g fat (16g sat. fat), 104mg chol., 327mg sod., 50g carb. (37g sugars, 1g fiber), 8g pro.

MAKE-AHEAD TIRAMISU

INSPIRED BY:
OLIVE GARDEN'S
TIRAMISU

This variation of the popular Italian dessert is so easy to assemble. It's convenient, too, because you can make it the day before your dinner party or potluck.
—Linda Finn, Louisville, MS

- -

PREP: 25 min. + chilling • **MAKES:** 12 servings

- ½ cup strong brewed coffee
- 2 Tbsp. coffee liqueur
- 16 oz. cream cheese, softened
- ⅔ cup sugar
- 2 cups sour cream
- ¼ cup 2% milk
- ½ tsp. vanilla extract
- 2 pkg. (3 oz. each) ladyfingers, split
- 1 Tbsp. baking cocoa

1. In a small bowl, combine coffee and liqueur; set aside.
2. In a large bowl, beat cream cheese and sugar until smooth. Beat in sour cream, milk and vanilla until blended.
3. Layer 1 package of ladyfingers in an ungreased 11x7-in. dish; brush with half of coffee mixture. Top with half of cream cheese mixture. Repeat the layers (dish will be full).
4. Cover and refrigerate 8 hours or overnight. Just before serving, sprinkle with cocoa.
1 PIECE: 321 cal., 21g fat (14g sat. fat), 100mg chol., 149mg sod., 24g carb. (14g sugars, 0 fiber), 6g pro.

STRAWBERRY SHORTCAKE CUPS

Taking a bite of strawberry shortcake is like tasting summer in a bowl. These little shortcakes, baked in a muffin tin, serve up perfect, single-size portions, ready to be topped with luscious fresh berries.

—Althea Heers, Jewell, IA

INSPIRED BY:
CALIFORNIA PIZZA KITCHEN'S
STRAWBERRY SHORTCAKE

PREP: 15 min. • **BAKE:** 15 min. + cooling • **MAKES:** 8 servings

- 1 qt. fresh strawberries
- 4 Tbsp. sugar, divided
- 1½ cups all-purpose flour
- 1 Tbsp. baking powder
- ½ tsp. salt
- ¼ cup cold butter, cubed
- 1 large egg, room temperature
- ½ cup whole milk
  Whipped cream

1. Preheat oven to 425°. Mash or slice the strawberries; place in a large bowl. Add 2 Tbsp. sugar and set aside. In another bowl, combine flour, baking powder, salt and remaining sugar; cut in butter until crumbly. In a small bowl, beat egg and milk; stir into flour mixture just until moistened.

2. Fill 8 greased muffin cups two-thirds full. Bake for 12 minutes or until golden. Remove from the pan to cool on a wire rack.

3. Just before serving, split shortcakes in half horizontally. Spoon berries and whipped cream between layers and over tops of shortcakes.

1 SERVING: 200 cal., 7g fat (4g sat. fat), 44mg chol., 372mg sod., 30g carb. (11g sugars, 2g fiber), 4g pro.

NICE & SOFT SUGAR COOKIES

The holiday season isn't complete without cookies, and these sweet sugar cookies are a perennial favorite. They can be cut into any shape and decorated any number of ways—children always have fun choosing their own designs.

—Cathy Hall, Lyndhurst, VA

- -

PREP: 45 min. + chilling • **BAKE:** 5 min./batch + cooling
MAKES: about 3 dozen

　1　**cup butter, softened**
1½　**cups confectioners' sugar**
　1　**large egg, room temperature**
1½　**tsp. vanilla extract**
2½　**cups self-rising flour**
ICING
2½　**cups confectioners' sugar**
　¼　**cup water**
　4　**tsp. meringue powder**
　¼　**cup light corn syrup**
　　Food coloring of choice
　　Colored sugar and sprinkles, optional

1. Cream butter and confectioners' sugar until light and fluffy; beat in egg and vanilla. Gradually beat in flour. Divide dough in half. Wrap each half in plastic; refrigerate 2 hours or until firm enough to roll.

2. Preheat oven to 375°. On a floured surface, roll each portion of dough to ³⁄₁₆-in. thickness. Cut with floured 3-in. cookie cutters. Place 2 in. apart on ungreased baking sheets. Bake until set, 5-7 minutes. Cool on pans 2 minutes, then remove to wire racks to cool completely.

3. Beat confectioners' sugar, water and meringue powder on low speed until blended; beat on high until soft peaks form, about 4 minutes. Add corn syrup; beat 1 minute.

4. Tint with food coloring as desired. (Always keep unused icing covered with a damp cloth; if necessary, beat again on high speed to restore texture.) Pipe or spread icing on cookies; decorate as desired. Let dry.

NOTE: As a substitute for 2½ cups of self-rising flour, place 3¾ tsp. baking powder and 1¼ tsp. salt in a 1-cup measuring cup. Add all-purpose flour to measure 1 cup; combine with an additional 1½ cups all-purpose flour.

1 COOKIE: 138 cal., 5g fat (3g sat. fat), 19mg chol., 150mg sod., 22g carb. (15g sugars, 0 fiber), 1g pro.

Recipe Index